human experience reminding us that we are deeply loved by God and never alone. He is With Us! The writing is both accessible and profound, making it a meaningful read for anyone on a journey toward greater emotional and spiritual health. It is a book you will mark up and want to share with others!"

– Lisa Thompson, Women's and Discipleship Pastor,
Bayside Church, Granite Bay

I0560461

We are often moved through story, and if this story moves you closer to Jesus, then you will have found the greatest gift too. This story that can be a movement toward your own deep life in God, that transcends all things. Being still with Him, and finding Him with you, that is the GIFT. An ocean front bench began this friendship for me...go find your bench, and may you find more of God along the way.

- Janelle McGuckin

endorsements for **THE GIFT OF WITH**

"The Gift of With reminds us that hope is found not in avoiding life's struggles, but in embracing them with faith. Janelle's strong, humble faith—as her pastor something I've always known her for—shines through every page, offering a must-read guide for finding the powerful presence of God in life's messiest moments."

– Ray Johnston, Lead Senior Pastor, Bayside Church

"This book is a breath of fresh air to anyone who is, well, human. Because it's a story of amazing stories you almost can't believe are true, scars that are hard to read about but which will feel so familiar to you, songs, in a way that will surprise you, and a Sacred bench, that will invite you in to a world you didn't even realize you needed to pass into but which you can visit any time. As someone who loves and respects vulnerability, authenticity and the power of the imperfect aspects of our life to inspire, I love this book! You will read it, and pass it on to the ones you love most!"

– Mark Clark, pastor, Bayside Church, author, *The Problem of Life*

"Janelle's book isn't a 'happily ever after' story; it's a 'happily even after' reminder that it's often the sorrows in life that teach us the greatest lessons. She invites each of us to benefit from the gift she was shown through her journey of hardship. This is more than just a memoir, it's a guide for anyone searching for hope amid life's uncertainties."

– Kevin Thompson, Teaching Pastor and Pastor of Married Life Bayside Church, author of *Stay In Your Lane* and *Friends, Partners & Lovers*

"The Gift of With is an emotionally raw and beautiful love story of walking with God through life's broken and beautiful places. Be warned, there are deep waters here, and your life will be much richer for swimming in them. Here is the radical gift of this book for those who doubt: the God of the universe desires to redeem your suffering and transform your life into what He always intended."

– Dr. Jeff Sullivan, Ph. D., ATC, Dean, College of Health Sciences, Point Loma Nazarene University

"The Gift of With invites readers to seek a life of gratitude, purpose and God's presence often found in the pain we so desperately want to avoid. Through honest reflection and vulnerability, scripture and personal stories, Janelle retells her personal journey of physical, emotional and spiritual healing while offering profound insights and practical ways to endure the hardest and loneliest of times we may find ourselves in. This book is filled with so much wisdom and insights about our

THE GIFT OF WITH

A Story of Finding the Life-Changing
Wonders of the With-God Life

by Janelle McGuckin

The Gift of With: A Story of Finding the Life Changing Wonders of the With-God Life

Published by Thrive Media

Cover Design & Typesetting © by Pressed Visuals, LLC

ISBN: 979-8-9880791-4-9

Printed in the United States of America

For Grace and Natalie

TABLE OF CONTENTS

INTRODUCTION

Let's go for a walk together. We can talk, and I can get to know you and hear a bit of your story before you hear some of mine. Don't just share the bigger events and places you've been, but the deeper story in your heart. I truly want to know what things make you laugh and cry, and what things you've been surprised by. I imagine we'd lean into each other to hear more closely, and we'd feel so grateful for the time to be together like this.

This story is meant to feel like that—like a walk with an old friend, or sitting across from each other at a café. When God pressed it on my heart to write and share my story this way, I hoped to stick to actual conversations like this, intimate and familiar. But over time, I realized it needed to be written down. I thought of writing it out for my daughters, whenever they decided to read it. Then someone encouraged me to imagine who God might need to read it. I couldn't stop thinking about telling His story the way it happened to and within me. It changed my life, and all my relationships, and who I am, and so much more. Even after all the struggle and heartache it brought, I found my friendship with Him is forever; finding that was like finding hidden **treasure**.

I suppose when you find the most amazing gift of your life, you want to share it with whomever is near you. You look for those on a similar journey, those who also know that seeking God is a brave work. Something makes us believe that in the finding, we might know pure joy and the kind of never-ending love where we can taste heaven, even on this side of it. I love the story of the Samaritan women in John's Gospel, who went back to her town and told her story of encountering Jesus and many became believers themselves. Not just because of her sharing her story, but they encountered the Presence of Jesus themselves and became *all-in* believers too. How I want to be her. How I want your heart to be known and loved as mine has been by this most loving and intimately personal Creator who still writes amazing stories as He has been for thousands of years.

One of my favorite books is *Gift from the Sea* by Anne Morrow Lindbergh. First published in 1955, its timeless beauty has made it beloved, selling millions of copies in dozens of languages. It takes its inspiration from the ocean, which has always been a soul space for me, too. I love the life story she wove on its pages. My hope is that this book will be like that one in some way to you, to inspire and draw you into closer friendship with God on your pilgrimage. My learnings along the way, as a nurse who became a patient, involved heartaches, brushes with death— and in the end— life, real life. If this is in your hands, know God has already seen fit to add several more chapters in my life, but this is the story that started me seeking for the True Treasure that others, ordinary seekers like me, have found. Those who have found the gift of learning to walk closely in friendship with God. The seeking and really finding the wonders of the *with-God* life in the joys and sorrows along the way.

Thank you for spending your time with me here.

CHAPTER 1

WITH ME IN STRUGGLE

When it feels like surgery, and it
burns like third degree,
And you wonder, what is it worth...

Switchfoot
"I Won't Let You Go"

They find a lump in my neck. I'm at my yearly female appointment absolutely no one looks forward to, and my doctor is being extra thorough today. She's checked for lumps in all the usual places and my neck is last—it's the first time I remember having my neck checked for lumps.

She zeros in on one spot and seems curious, but not concerned, even downplaying it as though it's perfectly normal, so I do, too. I leave the office and call Scott. We agree it's nothing to lose sleep over.

Months pass. After a few ultrasounds and a round of biopsies later, my doctors decide to just be cautious and

BUT I AM A NURSE WHO DOESN'T KNOW HOW TO BE A PATIENT.

make plans to remove it. I get scheduled for a lumpectomy in the operating room on the surgical floor of the hospital where I work. All reassurances from my doctors are that it will be very minor. Nothing to worry about, they say. But I am a nurse who doesn't know how to be a patient.

Being an optimist in a world that can get very real, very fast has trained me for survival. I know enough to avoid the dark place, whenever possible. As a medical professional for the past fifteen years, I've seen more of the dark than anyone should. I've learned to keep my heart calm in the face of the unknown tomorrow. Maybe if I don't believe it will be dark, it won't be. I find that hopeful-but-cautious space, the space where I won't get sucked down in the deep dark pit even though life has definitely brought dark pits before. Medical scares are common. False positives happen all the time. I hold it together by turning to do what I always do— helping others, taking extra careful care, and generally fixing those with greater needs than my own. And now that I'm *on* the gurney instead of beside it, I have to take my own medicine. Can I stay optimistic?

I do love my job. I work in the post-anesthesia care unit (PACU) where I get to wake patients up from surgery when they are in that blissful state of emerging from anesthesia. I give them medicine for their pain, help them breathe, and make sure they don't heave on me. I hold their hands and teach them how to function with their fresh scars. In nursing we call the PACU "the land of milk and honey," or "a place you go out to pasture." I've seen all the drama of being an ICU and ER nurse. I prefer this place. It's a much more controlled environment to be a nurse. Here, we joke that R.N. stands for, "Refreshments & Nerve Blocks." That's our formula, and we find joy in taking care of mostly pleasant, intoxicated people.

During the final days leading up to my surgery date for this mysterious lump, I keep myself sanguine with the busyness of my two young daughters and normal family life, wanting to protect their little hearts from fear and pain. I train my mind to stay on the lovely, even as fears start to creep in. I keep most of it to myself with family and friends as I don't want to bring undue attention or add drama to anyone's lives.

I've always been the mom who preserves control by minimizing, so unless you are bleeding profusely or have actual fever, you still go to work and school. Health care workers are the worst patients and parents to our sick kids. We've grown too accustomed to pain. It's our kids who walk around with broken bones for a week before we get them checked by a doctor. Ice and Band-Aids cure most injuries.

The day before surgery, I take off work, so I have time to get things in order. Recovery will take a few days, so I make sure the fridge and pantry are stocked up from Trader Joe's. My husband leaves for work at the

University early in the morning. I walk my oldest freckle-nosed daughter to kindergarten and drive my youngest blondie to preschool. I pause for an extra tight hug and kiss her goodbye at the classroom doors.

The sigh I let out as I watch them turn away tells me my insides are feeling more insecure than I've admitted. I've strived to keep the steadiness I've always shown them, tried to keep life feeling light and carefree. No need to unnecessarily burden them with worry; their childhood should be carefree, like mine was. But as I get back to my car, that pea-sized lump in my neck starts to feel more real and my heart pounds. I can't play the minimizing game forever. I sit there clutching the steering wheel and trying not to cry. I replay stories of patients I have cared for who were young and healthy and still got the bad news. I am having surgery tomorrow on a potentially cancerous tumor that might turn my world upside down. This is real.

I have a few spare moments in between my daily domestic-engineering duties, so I decide to go there—not the dark place, but to my happy place—the bench overlooking the ocean. It's the spot that's become my sacred rest where I first began to hear God's whispers to my soul. The unobstructed ocean view sets the scene and beckons me sit and be still. Ever since we moved to San Diego, it has become my reprieve from the busy, the only place I have found that makes my soul-aches feel tended. I don't need to bring anything except my honesty and my weighted-down heart. Today, I bring my pen and new red-foiled thin journal, and I plan to pour out my heart on its pages.

As I look out across those vast blue waters, I recount amazing encounters with God on this very bench. Sensing His strength and presence once again ever so near, I realize I've been holding my breath for weeks now. Ah, now I breathe in a greater fullness and calm at the beauty, connecting to a quietness deep within. The peace goes deeper than my fickle, troubled heart and calls my soul to respond as the song I sang every night over my girls as babies comes to mind. "Turn your eyes upon Jesus, look full in His wonderful face..." That is the more important reality than tomorrow's looming appointment, and I desperately need to keep my eyes on Him and not the turmoil inside.

...I DESPERATELY NEED TO KEEP MY EYES ON HIM AND NOT THE TURMOIL INSIDE.

The bench has become the best place for my eyes and heart to refocus. The warmth of the sun is like a faithful friend's company. But despite the sweet peace and calm in that moment, I also can't deny the urge to write down a sincere prayer that sounds like it could be my last... just in case, I guess. If something goes wrong, I know I'll wish I took the time. It happens. I know this.

Sitting still, I calm my mind. And then, I hear Him. A gentle breeze blows and covers me, over my whole being, soft, very present, and very real. He speaks; I write it down. Every sweet, tender, word. He whispers three times, "I am with you, I am with you, I am with you." What does that mean? Perhaps one reminder from God, Jesus, the Holy Spirit? It is not clear, but it is what I need to hear, and more importantly what I need to know and remember. He reminds me He is all powerful, my healer, what I need. He invites me to keep seeking Him and listening to His voice and ends with lovingly calling me by the name He gave me here a year ago almost to the day. It swells my heart to be reminded that He knows me so well, and better than I know myself.

When it's time to go, I leave the bench, still fragile, but filled. I carry on with my plans of preparation. Scott and I steal time at the end of the day at Torrey Pines, our favorite stop-to-watch-the-sunset spot. We talk about what tomorrow could bring, and about staying in the optimistic, light-filled place. We both have walked through much life pain already, broken families, deaths of parents, and ups and downs around us, and we find identity together in being the steady ones; the ones others count on to remain positive and hopeful, regardless of our feelings or circumstances. Battle scars are inevitable in this life, but we sit there with a determination to limit the wounds by navigating the coming steps carefully and confidently.

I see us at the starting line of a struggle to remain in control and as the day comes to a close, despite the pep talk and muscled determination to stay positive, the dark threatens to snuff out my light.

The night is a restless one as I frequently wake with fear of the unknown ahead. I try to stay rational, trusting

God and His love, but the dark place pulls me in with its taunts, breaking through with *what-ifs* that leave my heart pounding, my mind racing, and my stomach aching.

I toss, turn, and pray on repeat until dawn finally breaks. In the morning light, I busy myself to keep our life feeling normal, especially for our little girls, though nothing works. *Normal* has changed, and I feel like I'm trying to catch the wind. Four months of waiting and wondering, avoiding and staying busy, have culminated in this day when an inconclusive biopsy will finally get its conclusion.

The promise of knowing makes my heart calmer now, thank God. After wrestling my way through the night, I'm definitely ready to check this box and be done with it. I give my name at the surgery center and do more waiting. When it's finally time to head back, I try to be a good patient. I know all of this so well. I put my own blood clotting prevention gear on my legs, put on my hospital gown instead of my usual scrubs, tuck my hair into my blue party hat, and kiss Scott goodbye at the operating room door. All will be well.

I begin my countdown backward from ten. Breathe deeply. I think of my family. Scott. Sweet Grace. Joyful Natalie. The bench... I drift off quickly to the darkness closing in.

As I wake up in the recovery room, groggy, blurry eyed, weak voiced, I whisper to the nurse doing my job, "Is it cancer?"

She hesitates. I ask a second time.

"Yes." She doesn't look at me. She tries to carry on in her busy nurse tasks. My mind fights the blur, wanting to know what this means. She pauses by my gurney, "We will let the doctor tell you everything when you wake up a little more."

It's what we say when it's hard news. My heart constricts, then pangs again when my surgeon comes, tears in his eyes, to tell me the news himself. He stumbles over his words. The findings and his tears surprising even him, who has done this surgery thousands of times before.

Stunned is the only word to describe it. What I wrote in my journal the day before flashes up into my foggy mind; the words I heard take on new meaning now. God is with me strongly in the midst of my anesthetic cloud. Despite the stabbing pain of my neck incision, unexpected peace overwhelms me. I shed a tear. I have no way of knowing that this is just the beginning of the longest journey of my life.

I HAVE ALWAYS BEEN THE ONE FIXING, AND NOW I WILL NEED FIXING.

Rousing from the cloud, my thoughts swirl. I am in my thirties with two young daughters. Up to now, I've lived something of—what I thought was—a charmed life. Struggle has come, but I have always found ways to fix the ache and go back to my rose-colored world. I have always been the one fixing, and now I will need fixing.

A few hours before, I'd still had my comfortable routines. Taking the girls to school, updating our babysitter, even preparing thank you gifts for all the hospital staff... because health care workers really like treats. (Now you know, for the next time you have surgery.) Scott and I had both dismissed the possibility of this being serious and told our extended families we didn't need help. Scott. How will I tell him? I know that emotionally, he is already drained from the past few years, having followed God's prompting out of strategic big-business recruiting and toward philanthropy. The road of leaving his former predictable life behind to trust that God would provide has been a dry and wearying one. He is depleted; and, I am going to need him more than I ever have before.

I know he is in the waiting room by himself, likely busying himself with work calls and emails. Surely, he is growing more concerned as time stretches on. The look on his face when he enters my recovery room tells me the surgeon has delivered the update. He holds my hand, rubs my head, and puts on his strong smile. Scott has always been so good in crises, but I wonder if this will tip him over.

Eventually, nurses arrive to wheel me from an outpatient area to a regular hospital room for the night. A large bandage covers my neck incision, and it hurts to swallow or talk. The full weight of reality feels like it can wait a while longer, thanks to the anesthesia cocktail.

A few hours later, those little girls that make my heart burst show up at the end of my hospital bed. They've brought handmade notes our babysitter has helped them color. They're hesitant to come closer to the big white gauze on my neck, or maybe it's my pale, disheveled look, or just seeing weakness in their Mommy. But they dutifully climb up and pose for an awkward picture. We try our best to keep things light, but even at ages 5 and 7, they know. We say Mommy just had to have a little "bump" taken off her neck and will need to take some medicine now. We never use the C-word, probably as much for me as for them.

As I return home, trying to keep life in its comfortable routine for Grace and Natalie keeps us steady amidst the unknowns. We try to go back to the old normal as quickly as possible, despite adding a lot of doctors' appointments. Making phone calls to tell everyone fills me with dread, so Scott takes on that job, telling our dearest people that what we feared has now been confirmed. He absorbs the aches on the other end of the calls as a way of buffering me.

There is one call I alone need to make. I'll never forget the deep pain and tears in my Mom's voice, knowing how she wishes she could take this away.

Papillary thyroid cancer is pretty minor in the categories of scary cancers.

> "Thyroid cancer begins in the thyroid gland…part of the endocrine system, which regulates hormones in the body. It absorbs iodine from the bloodstream

to produce thyroid hormones to regulate
the body's metabolism."[1]

Survival rates are high, and it is considered curable. Most cancers are a marathon; this one is a sprint. Life is upside down for a few months, and then they say you can usually jump back into regular life with very little disruption. They say this is the *good cancer*, the one you want to get, like you have a choice. Nothing about this cancer seems good to me. But maybe I'm beginning to learn a new meaning of what truly is good.

The shock and reality return again the next week when the doctor takes the large dressing off my neck. I see for the first time the long incision that feels gigantic. When he hands me the mirror, the light and optimistic place I had started to go back to sinks to my feet and right out of my body. Dr. Kramer seems a little nervous to offer me the mirror, I manage to hold back from critiquing his surgical art, but this looks much worse than I imagined.

A long curve arcs across the base of my neck, bumpy, red, and terrifying. All the scars I had seen from thyroid surgeries were smaller or completely healed. I barely notice them. I know surgeons are perfectionists, so I smile and hand back the mirror. *This is not good, not normal, not pretty,* is all I can think. He tells me he is referring me to the best endocrinologist our hospital has to help continue the treatment ahead. I quickly leave, feeling fragile under the weight of realizing how much uncertainty still lies ahead

---

1   *https://www.cancer.net/cancer-types/thyroid-cancer/introduction*

I let myself cry just a little once I'm alone. I want to let no one see this pain. I'm home but the weight I'm trying to throw off won't lift. I try to pray and look up, but it still aches. I can't play the *glad game* anymore.

Later, Grace comes home from school and passes by me at the counter. She peeks back and says, "Oh Mom, you got your big Band-Aid off."

My heart feels a pang and then I give a half-forced smile, "Yes, I did. It is really big, isn't it?"

She ponders, looks at my face, glances at my neck, and back at my face. "Well, it looks like you just have another happy face." And she skips away.

I burst into an ugly cry, laughing through hot tears. She and Natalie eventually come back in with cherry red Mr. Sketch marker scars across the front of their own necks to match my new *happy face*. As I look at them, I'm six years old again, holding myself together for my own mom. What a gift, the pureness of their love for me. Of course, I have to snap a picture that will show up later in a photobook for the coffee table.

The way God sees me and knows me and is with me in this struggle is astounding—making light in my darkness, and happy faces from my scars. Yet what I thought would be a quick outpatient procedure, turned out to be much more involved. I'll require many more soul treatments as well. I can't know this yet, but in the days, weeks, and months ahead, I will find recovery on an ocean bench while sitting with the One who knows that the *real* healing I need is deeper than a surgeon's scalpel can reach. I will soon find the inescapable *withness* of God in ways I'd thought were set aside for ancient saints, or maybe the twelve disciples. I'm clueless about the work that is really being done in me, but this is where the real journey begins.

CHAPTER 2

WITH ME IN ISOLATION

So when hard times have found you
and your fears surround you
Wrap my love around you,
you're never alone.

Lady A
"Never Alone"

I leave another doctor's appointment with strict instructions to not eat food containing iodine for the next two weeks. Seems easy. How much iodine can I possibly be consuming anyway? This is to prepare my body for the treatment to zap the remaining cancer cells. Thyroid cells, for some unknown reason, like iodine. So the right ones need to be starved of it and radiated to die.

While grocery shopping, every nutrition label I look at has salt, soy, or dairy, which are on the banned high-in-iodine list. I am starting to get grumpy-hungry after looking at every product ingredient list, which basically suggests I should only eat raw fruits, raw veggies, and unsalted nuts for the next two weeks. I do not want this diet, this Daniel-like fast, but it was doctor-directed, so I'm determined to follow the rules. If I do, then they say this should all go away, and I can check all the boxes and get on with the life I love.

Come on, how difficult could this be? I pull back out my Pollyanna boots. This won't be so bad. But just as I dip into some healthy hummus and look at the ingredients, bam. *Salt.* So much for grabbing a quick snack for the road, scooping peanut M&M's from the candy bowl, or going out to dinner with friends after soccer practice. Maybe hunkering down in a cave for two weeks would be the easiest option.

Scott is supportive and compassionate, but he's not partaking in this diet alongside me. Purging iodine to starve the mutant thyroid cells of hunger, leaves me weak and empty. Going to every specialty store in the area to find foods without iodine is a total bust. It's raw or nothing. The body cleanse is beginning, and soon the soul cleanse is coming.

I begin a season of picking up the pieces of me that have cracked as I try to return to normal, just with a red, bumpy scar on my neck. Going back to work amid new appointments and treatments helps keep my focus on helping others instead of myself. I have a lot of self-preservation habits that need to be replaced with healthier ones, but I'm able to keep that larger struggle at bay for now. Self-reliance is easy and prized and wins you praise. I have found my way to survive well here. It's part nature, part nurture, but in nursing, as in many jobs, the fewer personal needs you acknowledge, the better you can work. This only further feeds my appetite for independence. However, I sense God gently clipping away at some things with His pruning shears. At 38, some unruly branches of mine have needed major pruning.

With thyroid cancer you get to meet the mysterious nuclear medicine doctors. In 15 years of being a nurse, I never interacted with these specialists. Usually in nursing you know who all the best of the best providers are. In fact, if you want a good doctor or referral you can count on, always ask the nurses who work with them. In this case, these docs do not work with nurses, so I had never met them. It sounds more special military ops than medical, but this is real. They actually have offices in the basement of the hospital, right next to the morgue.

I wasn't sure where these doctors might land on a Strengths Finder Test, but they soon become my new best friends. Looking over pathology reports and calendars, my doctor explains he will soon dispense some, "… nuclear run-off," to me in a pill form.

Gulp. My next appointment will be timed with a highly regulated airplane that will deliver my radiation in an air-tight canister. I start to understand why we're in the basement next to the morgue. I'm intrigued and mortified at the same time. I think, *"OK, so I am going to swallow this nuclear waste, it will kill cancer in my body, then I will be isolated for a week, and I will have scans and follow-*

ups, and then go back to my normal life. Huh." I know there's something he's not telling me. *"Will this make me a Walking Dead zombie? Whoa, deep breath. OK, this is fine. I can do this. I am pretty sure I am still holding my breath."*

I do ask him if my teeth are going to fall out. He gives a mad-scientist chuckle and assures me that no, they won't. That's good. Feeling like a HAZMAT project, I decide to jump in with both feet. I am ready to be on the other side of this thing for my young precious daughters, for my soulmate, and for my own mental health. I have no idea God is just beginning to write a much bigger story than a single X-Files episode—one that will soon change my mindset from running a sprint to entering a marathon.

I GET SO STUCK IN MY HUMANITY THAT I FORGET A BIGGER PLAN IS ALMOST ALWAYS UNFOLDING WHEN I'M LOOKING DOWN INSTEAD OF UP.

During the next two weeks of eating, not for comfort but for preparation, I begin another kind of self-emptying. I'm quick to deny that food is a god in my life, but when forced to strip away foods I love, I begin to see the truth. It affects my pace of life, and I now have to plan ahead. No grab-n-go snacks are on the list. It affects my mood, if I don't eat those raw fruits and vegetables every hour, I'm grumpy and hungry. Food consumes an enormous amount of my thoughts and feelings, which then affects everything else.

I make an early connection as I start acknowledging my feelings with the Lord. "I'm hungry," I tell Him. It's like needing more frequent servings of God throughout my day, rather than expecting one meal to last for a day. It affects my strength and energy. I am more needy than I ever like to be. I am getting weaker to get stronger. Just one of the many needed refining works of God's hand. Answers to our prayers for my healing are already coming, just in ways I hadn't thought or imagined. I get so stuck in my humanity that I forget a bigger plan is almost always unfolding when I'm looking down instead of up.

I begin to plan my solo getaway. I have not been away from my little family for more than one night before now. But thanks to friends at our nearby university, and God's fathering provision, an ocean view suite awaits me. One of my dear friends says I'm going from living every mom's nightmare to getting every mom's dream. I see her point, but as I tuck away in a space normally reserved for vacations, hanging the *Do Not Disturb* sign will feel like a warning, not a polite request.

The plan is to ingest the Erin Brockovich material and immediately start isolation for almost a week. The six day isolation treatment plan requires distancing oneself six feet from others (pre-Covid days when that was not well understood), true isolation, bring in all your own food, eat only on paper plates, supply my own towel and bedding, flush the toilet three times to send the radiation down the lines diluted (seriously!), and make sure I do not contaminate anyone with my radioactive body. How can I be so harmful to everyone else but not myself? I still think about my teeth falling out. Will I crumble into a heap of ash after I take this pill? They used to put patients in a hospital lead lined isolated room, but I will happily take this retreat over that option, even if I am alone.

Isolation. There is a cold, lonely feeling in this word. *Is this one of my core fears? Being alone?* It's shedding to travel down that road, peeling back the onion of my own heart to face reality head on. The shedding of cancer cells mirrors the work on my own self-reliance getting stripped away.

A few days before taking my special pill I receive a few extra injections to make my body ready to absorb as much of the cancer-killing drug as possible. Finally, the morning of nuclear medicine arrives, and I open up the window shades. A double rainbow stretches out high in the sky, right over the sparkling ocean. Bright metal street lights and neighboring houses are squeezed in beneath. It's radiant. The rainbow speaks a promise to me that later I'll realize is also a gift, training my eyes to see beyond the man-made ugly that blinds me up close, to look to the Creator. It takes my breath away. I can't help but remember the One who put it there. It's just for me, and I feel Him already with me.

Before leaving for the hospital for the treatment, I get the doctor's report that the cancer has spread beyond the anticipated margins; and, it's more advanced. They tell me it just means I need a higher dose of that cancer-killing medicine, but every nurse knows what, "... not clear margins," means. I have a minor meltdown that day in the kitchen pantry. Tears I've held in come out anyway, and they won't stop.

I think of those fixer-upper shows we watch and it's like demo day around here. My *fixer-upper* is my own body... and my terrified little soul.

Scott escorts me to the hospital dungeon to start this cancer cleansing treatment. I see no one in a space suit, so I think I may be okay. It's like being on a plane in crazy turbulence—if the flight attendants are calm, it helps you believe all is well.

My nuclear medicine doctor meets me with the lead-lined canister. I'm expecting it to start smoking when he opens it, but it's just a tiny white pill with a lot of foam padding around it. He asks me to pull it out and take it with the glass of water on the counter. Trusting this is what is required, I drink from the cup and pray it does its healing work. Then we get up and leave like we've just dined at one of those chic restaurants where they serve teensy-tiny portions, and you quickly make plans to stop at In-N-Out on your way home. Only there's no In-n-Out for me.

We walk up the stairs from the hospital dungeon and out to the car, to take the drive to the hotel on the bay. I'm not quite dangerous to be around yet, but I feel a little toxic on the inside. I remain quiet for most of the drive, not sure how to process my thoughts. We check me into my room for the week. I think Scott makes about ten trips from the car to the room to bring in all the care packages and gifts from our village which are meant to keep me buoyed while I am in isolation. We exchange an awkward goodbye hug at the door, navigating an attempt at tenderness while minimizing actual contact. The door closes and I feel the weight of my aloneness.

I'm already exhausted and turn on Food Network. It creates a strong longing for all the high-iodine food I dream of eating soon. But a wave of nausea soon comes, so I turn off the TV and fall asleep.

A few hours later, I wake and remain lying still. It is quiet, calm and peaceful. The room has almost a sacred feel, like I'm being shown something that's been hidden from me in my busy day-to-day. It's so strong, I don't even want to turn the cooking show back on for company. *Can a hotel room be a sanctuary?* I suppose it is possible.

The effects of the nuclear waste in my body are starting. Someone's put 100 cotton balls in my mouth. I'm weak and queasy. Yet I lay there soaking in a peace which I cannot explain. Just before this forced solitude retreat, a book arrived in the mail from my Mom's best friend. Her son, a dear childhood friend, recently edited a book he said was one of the best he's ever read. I received an early copy, before the book releases and becomes beloved to the world. Its message, on the power of gratefulness, is perfect. I have all week to absorb it; and, in its poetic, beautiful way, it encourages me to see that gratitude can come not only through happiness and bliss, but also through struggle and even through the darkness. It feels like another great gift—a heart transformation comes to me in this shift—and the message sinks deep into my heart. I begin writing my own thankfulness list that very night, starting my own One Thousand Gifts List—thank you, dear Ann.

And a feeling I can only describe as joy starts to flow in like a cool breeze. *This* is what brings healing. He brings the eyes to see when I start to *want to* see, when I'm able to take the time to see. The room with the view, the double rainbow in the sky, the support and love of dear friends, family, neighbors, strangers, skilled doctors, the ability to FaceTime virtual kisses to my little family, happy faces with Mr. Sketch markers, a husband who is in it with me, "... for better or worse." All of this is on the list. In this solitude, my true rest starts.

Have you ever felt like once you start looking for something, every song, every book, every email, every billboard, every little rock on the ground somehow points you to the same message? I am not sure if I miss this most days because of being busy or distracted, or if Ann Voskamp's book is just God's amplification to my deaf ears, but in this quiet hotel room the megaphone is loud and clear. At every turn, from music to reading, to watching sunsets, it all points

OH, PRUNE MY HEART, LORD, OF SELF-RELIANCE AND OF PRIDE, OF TRYING TO HOLD TOO MUCH IN MY OWN STRENGTH, AND AVOIDING THE DEEPER TRUTH OF YOUR INFINITE LOVE FOR ME.

me to the *True Vine*.[2] I am, as incredible as it sounds, abiding with Him (The Vine), and I (The Branch) in this waiting place undergoing pruning to eventually become more fruitful.

I sense the pruning as afternoon slowly turns to evening. The divine shears are out, and it is painful. But I can see I've needed this. *Oh, prune my heart, Lord, of self-reliance and of pride, of trying to hold too much in my own strength, and avoiding the deeper truth of your infinite love for me.* I pray I'm finally learning to surrender and drink more from His living water. I feel thirsty in every way. I decide I am going for the Mega Big Gulp from His soul-filling river. Like the woman at the well who found Him and didn't thirst anymore.[3]

Gosh, I am a terrible receiver. I would much rather be the giver. It sounds so nice of me, but I see the root of this is ugly pride in my uneasiness with being needy. I have not been living surrendered and open. But here, this time, I have nothing to give. I have nothing to do but learn to receive grace. His gifts with no strings... freely given. The gift is this very room, a sanctuary for the presence of God. It is here. It's nothing I can see with my eyes, but I sense it deep in my quaking soul and the strong feeling of not being alone.

This is the greatest gift—like when David writes about being in the valley of the shadow of death and having no fear knowing God is with him.[4] *This* is what

---

2   *John 15:1-17*

3   *John 4:13*

4   *Psalm 23*

brings comfort and takes away fear. God *with* me. As I've always been told, but never quite experienced for myself, at least not like this, in a daily and hourly experience; I am never alone. It's the peace and calm that comes when you are with a dear friend. He is quenching my thirst by settling my fears with His peace.

My fears of a toe tag dissipate with being still and *knowing* God is with me in this place. Maybe that's what the whisper was the day before the surgery on the sacred ocean bench: "I am with you, I am with you, I am with you." I guess I needed to hear it three times to believe it was true. Growing up in a loving Christian home, I thought I knew all about grace. I have

I DON'T WANT NORMAL.

tasted it before, but this is flooding my heart in a way I can't deny; a way that is changing me. Maybe this knowledge is finally going from my head to my heart. The craving for this divine presence only builds as the week progresses, replacing my desire to *just get back to normal*. I don't want normal.

I recall a tour we took a few years prior through a beautiful, green Napa vineyard. My detailed, inquisitive husband asked the expert vintner how much irrigation was needed to produce the best grapes. Scott loves anything to do with weather, and actually tracks and obsessively checks the Weather Channel app. No kidding, he knows the annual rainfall totals in random US cities. The vintner told us the more the vine had to struggle for water, the better the fruit it produced. It would put its roots down in the soil deep enough to find a water source, but if the vines were given too much irrigation, the grapes were less flavorful and produced a weaker vine. Vintners also have to prune branches which aren't producing good grapes, so the vine can focus its energy where it is most needed.

This knowledge comes flooding back into my heart and mind in a moment: I'm learning to lean more into the Tender of my soul. To stay and rest there, I need to find my water source. This time I'm not finding it in a church, or a book, or a small group. I'm lying still in this hotel sanctuary. There's no place to go, no person to talk to. It's just me and my radiated body on a hotel room bed.

Despite every effort on my own, I've finally stilled. And He comes to me here when I am in desperate need of water and food, when He knows that now I can finally appreciate what His living water, His bread of life, really is to me.

CHAPTER 3

WITH ME IN DISAPPOINTMENT

Won't take nothing but a memory
From the house that built me.

Miranda Lambert
"The House That Built Me"

I've always been drawn to simplicity even though my normal life reflects more of a frenzy. I fill my days with so many good things, only when forced, do I embrace it and see it has roots to a deeper longing in my heart. I have been asking mentors in my life for several years why they think keeping a Sabbath is the only one of the Ten Commandments our Christian culture so habitually overlooks. We need rest, stillness, simplicity and my only Sabbath seems to be a few moments in the quiet of the early morning to connect with Jesus as manna for the day. I am learning that I need more.

So, I guess this forced rest inside the sanctuary of a hotel room is becoming more of a dream than a nightmare. I still have desperate prayers for bodily healing, but I can see glimpses of the deeper, more needed healing coming. I really am a mess, and now I am seeing I've been in a fog, thinking life was fine and all put together with a nice bow on top.

This nuclear medicine makes my salivary glands feel like they're withering up. Over the next few days my mouth becomes a desert and I am so, so thirsty. I read about the Samaritan woman at the well who was given water that made her thirst no more (John 4:14). I pop lemon drops, sip sparkling water, and look out the window at the smooth waters of the bay. Sailboats drift by, birds soar and sing from the balcony, then eat seeds in the grass below. He provides for the sparrow, and I believe He cares much more for me. I can feel it, I know it. This is real. This thirst for more of Him and less of me transcends my physical reality.

Moments from life—what I've learned to be true and what I had thought to be true—start playing out in my head. I've lived a proportionally faithful life, devoted to a God I've believed in since young childhood. I found it so easy to believe He was good, and all of life had been happy up to my first decade and a half. But now, alone and undistracted, the darker memories are becoming impossible to ignore.

As a 4-year-old, I raised my hand in church to ask Him into my heart, but got it pulled down by my attentive mom who thought I might be too young to understand.

I insisted and she relented. I began getting to know Him from sermons and Bible stories at our growing church. In the easy belief of my suburban life, I got to know the Christian checkboxes. You know, if you do this, this, and this, you are good to go. A+B=C. Follow the four steps, and all will be well. Why do we think we can institutionalize and strategize what life with Jesus should look like?

WHY DO WE THINK WE CAN INSTITUTIONALIZE AND STRATEGIZE WHAT LIFE WITH JESUS SHOULD LOOK LIKE?

This new experience of deep real life struggle is unraveling the too-easy, unexamined life. Following God in our move from homes and jobs in recent years, navigating parenthood, a new cancer diagnosis, prodigal family members, new struggles in our marriage, and emotional unhealthiness coming to the surface were signs of the unraveling. The Christian life formula was coming apart, taking me down an unknown path. And in the dim light, the scariness of detaching from the *good life*, the blessed path I thought I was on, was suffocating me.

From the outside, my childhood was Mayberry. I had the *Leave it To Beaver* life: two kids, two dogs, two cars, and two parents who adored me. Snacks were always on the counter when I got home from my private school. We took summer family vacations every year, even the year dad lost his business and we stayed at a loaned lake house instead of a week in Hawaii. Long summer carefree days in the Central Valley heat, cooling off in the big pool my professional pool-installer dad dug in the backyard of our 1920's Tudor house. I soaked up the long summer days of snow cones at California Ice on as many days as my allowance would stretch. Enjoying the carefree kid life by agreeing to play G.I, Joe action figures with my older brother, and always trying to talk him into playing Barbies with me after, but somehow he never played Barbies with me, and somehow I never caught on.

At church each week, Mom led Sunday school, and Dad was an elder who was there anytime the doors were open. We'd help the janitor put away the folding chairs for a chocolate fudge bar from the church office freezer.

On Christmas Eve all the grandparents, aunts, uncles, cousins, and even the black-sheep-of-the-family uncle who drove a Harley and was a Hell's Angel would come. He didn't quite fit in the picture-perfect setting, but we held a seat for him at the table.

Mom kept a perfectly tidy house with everything homemade and from the farmer's market or local orchards. Growing up around families who were peach and nut farmers made my childhood somewhat utopian.

At eleven years old, I decided I wanted to be a nurse when I grew up. It was between that or being a travel agent, eager to help people get well or explore the world. I still wonder if maybe those dreams will merge someday. I was the kid to rush for ice or a Band-Aid when someone was hurt. It felt good to fix, to help. It still does.

That was also the year I colored a picture and wrote a letter to President Ronald Reagan to let him know I was praying for him. He wrote me back, real signature and all. I was so excited to get a letter, especially one with a return address that said only, "The White House." Things progressed into the awkward junior-high years with big hair perms and jean jackets. I got in trouble a few times at school for chewing gum, throwing water balloons at the boys, and peeling paint from the bathroom walls (along with all 30 girls of the 7th grade class). And, I snuck in a few last times playing with dolls and Barbie before crossing over the *too old* line.

Then came the first boyfriend—sweet and innocent but also tangled and smothering. (A few years later he would introduce me to the high school sweetheart I eventually married. Funny how unexpectedly God works.) Each summer, I'd spend a week at Hume Lake church camp and found a new crush. I'd find a taste of a larger, more active God there, too. The mountain-top experience was sweet and real. But down the mountain, He'd return to being just a piece of my life that I could tap into for a quick-fix prayers and platitudes.

At age 15 I confirmed my nursing pursuits when I diagnosed myself with appendicitis before asking to be taken to the ER. That was an easy fix, and a small scar no one would ever see.

That same year my brother had emergency surgery to repair his unrecognizable face that had been crushed in a water ski accident. His model-like face looked like Rocky Balboa's final round, or maybe the Elephant Man. I wrestled with God about it, because it didn't fit my worldview. But he healed, and life returned to what felt normal, for a short time.

Then a real struggle finally came. My grandma, who taught me to play Cribbage, who I'd dyed Easter eggs with each year, who made the best root beer floats, and who took me to convalescent hospitals to visit the lonely, lovely people, died unexpectedly. It spun our family into a tailspin. She'd been the matriarch who brought everyone together with her laugh and her strong value of family. She was a terrible cook, but we still gathered for family dinners just to be together. She could rescue anyone from a sticky situation. Though she had her own struggles, like being a closet cigarette smoker, she'd brought enduring stability when things felt fragile.

With little-to-no discussion about her passing, I struggled to find God's hand in our lives and felt my sense of equilibrium waning. After a few days of initial mourning, we all simply kept marching on, but it was a gut-wrenching, deep grief that left us privately reeling. The rug our family had lived and played on was ripped out from under us, and no one knew quite where to land. The world I had known began unraveling. As I left for college, my brother's girlfriend got some news... she was pregnant. My parents decided to try and help, so she moved in. But, it came at a cost. Later, I'd learn my Mom was also just beginning to deal with unresolved pain from abuse as a child. Dad became busier building his business and winning golf tournaments. Then, Mom went back to salon work for the first time in years. Meanwhile, church friends who had become like family turned their backs on us, and my *Leave it to Beaver* world turned into *Days of Our Lives*. The idea of grace I'd received at church turned out to be more of a *behavior management* gospel, with a series of boardgame moves that clearly were not working anymore.

Feeling shunned by our church, we stopped attending. I began to feel even more adrift and disconnected from my former sources of security. I'd eventually come to understand that checkboxes don't let you find the full freedom of God. They only promise a taste of it and rob you of the meal. But I felt myself grasping for that familiar safe world that had at least *felt* like Eden. Maybe now the apple had been bitten, and I had to accept life had changed.

Such pain and chaos had never fit in my theology, or my picture of growing up in a Christian home in America. If you asked God into your heart and followed His commands, life was supposed to be safer, easier, full of happiness, and with minimal heartache.

But, where had I learned this? Where do any of us learn it?

The Bible is full of stories of people who are *all in* for God, and yet struggle, and suffer, and get beheaded. But we still decorate our baby rooms with scenes of the divine genocide recorded in Genesis, and we trick ourselves into ignoring the real implications of the story by focusing on cute little animals coming two by two. That was how I had been taught, to try to keep things rosy. And so, I grew determined to make it rosy again.

I went off to go make my own new Eden in college. The view was Edenic enough, on the ocean cliffs of San

Diego. That sweetheart I'd met just months before was also going to be there, unplanned, but orchestrated. The promise of adventure and excitement abounded, but I was also leaving my predictable, safe life I'd always known.

I cried nearly every day that first year. Certainly not for trading valley life for beach life, but for the *perfect* life I thought was slipping away. No one cared that I'd been a popular, all-star athlete and high achiever in high school. The things I'd based my identity on were gone, and now everyone was on leveler ground than me. My outer layer peeled away and beneath wasn't so glamorous. At least I still had my great family, an amazing boyfriend, and God to watch over me.

Dorm life fostered new friendships with other carefree spirits like me. But unlike most of my pre-nursing classmates, I wanted to find my way back to a more whimsical and Pollyanna life again, not just compare grades on the pharmacology test printed and taped to the nursing building windows. I definitely had to have my head in the books—many long days in the library—but my sanguine nature drew me to play as much as I could squeeze in.

Starting new pages in the story of my life felt freeing. Even reading in freshman psychology the first words of M. Scott Peck's *The Road Less Traveled,* "Life is difficult," I felt such a sense of freedom in that simple truth. I'm not sure I had enough perspective to really believe his premise yet: could life be full and good even if it was difficult? But amidst the struggle was splendor.

Everything was new; the world was opening up, and life-long friendships were blooming. I began blazing my own trail away from home.

It was Christmas break, home from my second year of college, that the first true dark night of the soul descended. Mom and Dad had grown distant from each other and from God. The rules of religion they'd been living by had surfaced a hidden emptiness. I knew Mom was trying to heal on her own, and Dad was unsuccessfully trying to fix something broken inside his own soul. In the other room, arguing, I heard Dad say, "Let's try to work it out for the kids," and it sent me to my knees to pray. Face down, I made my most earnest plea, tears streaming, knot in my stomach, aching for God to save my parents... to save our family.

Then it all went silent. I got up to see why, hardly knowing what I was doing. I slowly walked to the kitchen. Heart beating fast, eyes wide open, I felt I was entering a war zone where a bomb had gone off and the threat of further collapse was heightened with each step. Mom couldn't talk and lay in a fetal position. Breathing, but unable to talk, her eyes slowly blinked. It sent me into high alert. Dad paced, starting to panic. I could not understand what I was seeing, but I sensed the darkness, an unseen battle being fought. I knew Mom needed to feel safe.

I went into medic mode and called her dear friend who had led her to Christ many years before, but she wasn't at home. I tried a coworker at the salon who came and helped Mom get up from the couch and walk out the front door. She left with only a small bag. Everything else, photo albums, dishes, 28 years of marriage stayed behind in the home she was abandoning.

I sensed Dad was aware he was losing any control he might have had over saving their marriage. But whatever else was psychologically going on, I felt the years of unresolved hurt, pain, and memories pressing us down, smothering the words. I kept thinking God would come through for me and they would get back together in a few days. I would hear conversations replaying in my head, "You never have to worry about Mom and Dad getting a divorce." I'd hung on to that, believing it was true. It'd kept my heart afloat. But now Mom had left. The once rosy world was nothing but decay.

Going back to college without staying to help fix my parents ripped out whatever was left of my broken heart. I tried to escape to my not-quite-adult world and pretend my former life could still recover. At least it was better than staying home with everyone I ever knew asking what happened to the Cleavers. No one in my new college life even knew the Cleavers. When you've always found so much of your support and identity in being the rock-solid, fun family, the shame of accepting the truth or even talking about it terrified me. Soon I'd find out that shame can be a hidden pride, covered in your own heart.

I tried joining a college church group. The first night, as the sharing of prayer requests began, others shared about painful toenails, or their goldfish dying, or their neighbor's-cousin's-friend's-friend who was a little sick. I'm exaggerating, of course—but compared to the reality

WITH ME IN DISAPPOINTMENT

of my world being in shambles, everything else seemed painfully trivial. I couldn't share this.

The pastor-leader said, "I feel like there's one more person who needs to share."

No. Certainly not. This was way too personal.

Someone else shared something, but then the leader said it again, "One more person."

I sat there, heart pounding hard in my chest. He didn't mean me. Someone else shared again. *Whew.* Then, he said it a third time. The pause seemed to go on forever. I gripped my chair, wrestling my pride. I didn't know these people. They didn't know me. No one said another word. Finally, he prayed, and I felt like Peter after the rooster had crowed (Luke 22:61).

I began to tremble, convicted at letting what felt like pride win out. Not that it would have changed the outcome of my circumstances, but sharing could have invited others into my pain. I saw Jesus looking at Peter with those sad eyes after his third denial, and it changed me, like it did him. Life is difficult. Maybe they wouldn't have understood. But I knew I needed to empty out my broken heart, and the pain that was right beneath the surface.

Afterward, my best friend sitting next to me asked if I was okay. I told her I wasn't and tried to explain the ache. This was so big and new for me. She listened and hugged me and didn't judge or get ashamed for not knowing what to say. I felt released of what was required of me in that test. Free to learn to let safe people in, people who loved me, people who wanted to know my heart—the good, the bad, the ugly.

Seeking to be real with Him in this way too, letting Him in and not just living with a checkbox of duties. He'd always felt safe and I longed to feel that pre-sheltered life I knew as a child.

After we got back to campus, I went to the nearby ocean cliffs hoping—no, needing—to find He might really be a Friend, a Father. Sitting there with waves crashing and the vast beauty, I could feel He'd been waiting for me to meet Him there. He wasn't just with me in the disappointment and heartache, He was the way *through* it. I dumped it all out—all these new feelings and fears, all this work of studying hundreds of pages of medical-surgical nursing textbooks, the mess of everyone around me. I wouldn't make it without Him. I wouldn't want to. He said I didn't have to.

The rest of the year was a blur, like walking through life in a fog and waking up on the other side. The semester ended, and I was going back home to the mess to help pick up the pieces. That is what nurses do: we fix, we help, we assess, we comfort, and we support. It's not as complicated to do for someone else as for ourselves.

Mom now had her own apartment down the street, but I felt distance and awkwardness growing between us. Disappointment and confusion ran deep about who my parents were, what they'd taught me, and what they now believed. Dad was wounded, but finally going to counseling. I tried to go too, but it felt like the *Twilight Zone*, with a large fish tank distracting me. And the doctor reminded me of Willy Wonka with a tremor. All that semester, I was wide-eyed and shell-shocked. That amazing boyfriend was my best therapist. He had been through this too, twice. Poor guy, he thought dating me was going to bring the Cleaver family he had always longed for. But feeling known and loved was so healing for me, and I found hope in imagining what our life could be together, since the life I knew had disappeared.

Meanwhile, the soap opera of my life started ramping up the drama. Mom started dating a wealthy cowboy who used language like a sailor, and soon they were moving into a ranch house together. My mom, with her perfect hairdo and acrylic nails, was ribbon roping in the dirt at rodeos. She'd always had a way of moving forward to the next chapter of life without a blip. She carried on with the family celebrations and holidays, feigning something almost normal.

Dad, on the other hand, was going for plastic surgery on his eyelids, supposedly to attract the younger ladies, conveniently just a few months before the bachelor fashion show he was in. He still made a point to say hello to people wherever he went, and though he didn't let many know his true heart, he still had his friendly, town-mayor charm. Through this struggle to reinvent and continue on, we began a new friendship of deeper understanding.

Compartmentalized addictions had finally surfaced, and more of the unraveling of our old life started to make more sense. Realizing it was normal in the transition from childhood to adulthood, to see the ground shifting and being brought more level with my parents was not easy. My education in all of this was especially abrupt as the pedestal on which I had put them toppled over. The ripple effects of divorce never fully resolve or go away until the other side of heaven.

I remember the ethics class with Dr. Reed holding space to sift through what my heart really believed. He was one of those saints I knew really walked with God. He

GOD IS REAL, BUT HURT WAS ALSO REAL.

was also a brainiac who read 300 books a year, walked to the campus each day from his television-free home, memorized his 45-minute messages as the chaplain, and counseled my hurting heart in his class lectures. This world-shake-up forced me to question everything I believed and knew to be real. God is real, but hurt was also real. I began believing more and more that eternity is set in our hearts as I continued to long more for Eden.

I remember the beach wall where Scott and I would sit most weekends and look across the bay at the city lights. We sipped on mint mochas from Kensington Cafe across the street. Cheap dates, coffee with a million-dollar view, and priceless conversations. We dreamed about where we would live and what jobs we would have. When he would move on to dreaming about cars with specific features, I would usually fall asleep. I was a chronically fatigued nursing student and even a double shot of espresso couldn't keep me awake once the subject turned to cars.

One summer night before our last year of college, we went to that beach wall. A turn in the tide came when he got down on one knee and asked if I would be his bride. I said, "Yes," to him and gained a new sparkle on my finger. Of course, he recorded it all on the advanced cassette tape he'd brought along, because this was the early 90's, and that's all we had. Life was hopeful again... full of new beginnings.

Yet, some of the new beginnings, I couldn't embrace. My mom also got engaged to the cowboy who didn't know God. It's a crazy thing to call your mom to say you found the perfect invitations and hear her say she's also found invitations for her upcoming wedding. The wind in the sails can go a bit limp. How do you keep putting one foot in front of the other when each turn kicks you in the stomach again? Still struggling some with the shame, I was insistent to have only my parents' name on our wedding invitation, even though Mom would already be married to a new man. Meanwhile, Dad was seriously dating a woman who could have been my older sister. I was still clinging to what I'd wanted my life to be, but wasn't, and never would be.

The wedding day arrived a month after graduation, and while I felt young, there was no doubt it was real love. I was ready to leave the drama and cleave to this knight in shining armor. Even in the difficulty and disappointment, we never questioned if our life together would end up the same way as our parents'. We had invited God into our friendship and love, and by His grace maintained our commitment to our values up to the I do's. It was a magical day. As Dad walked me down the aisle, he choked up telling me I was everything he prayed I would be. He adored my choice of a husband. I sensed a holy presence during the communion. A gentle breeze blew through as everyone celebrated at the dreamy vineyard in the foothills. My maid of honor's toast to "getting everything on my future-husband-wish-list" I'd had as a young girl, was true: God was bringing His restoration. And I was just beginning to taste it.

More restoration was coming through intentionally shifting from disappointment to gratitude. For Mom's 50th birthday, I listed 50 things I loved about her. It didn't change my fragmented family tree, but it changed my heart and healed many hurts which hid so many gifts she's given me. My idealistic, Pollyanna life was blossoming again. *"... there is something about everything that you can be glad about, if you keep hunting long enough to find it."* *(Pollyanna,* by Eleanor H. Porter, p. 41)

Soon after, at that birthday celebration for my mother, we sat with my childhood pastor who mentioned he had just read a book that was one of the best he had read in ten years. Wanting to soak up any wisdom I could in my soap opera life, I craved life-giving words for my soul. That is what *Windows of the Soul* was for me. It was one of the first works I had come across that showed what life *with* God could look like. Not a compartment called Spiritual Life but woven into life's everyday moments.

When you believe in God all your life, and go to a Christian school and college, it seems you should know what it looks like to walk with God in the moments of your days. But, I didn't. I am *still* learning this art and practice. Like most Christians in America, for me it was always a few minutes squeezed into a full, loud day to have *quiet time* with God, or sometimes not even that. Maybe hearing a good sermon on the weekends would stir something for a day or two. **GOD WAS LIKE A REALLY NICE HANDBAG THAT I COULD CARRY AND REACH INTO IF NEEDED.** God was like a really nice handbag that I could carry and reach into if needed. But this book opened up a piece of my soul that had been dormant. I had lived in the boundaries of the rules, surviving on only the appetizers faith offered. Finally, I felt like I was tasting the main course. And, I began to crave more.

Now here in the isolation of the hotel room, I realize how much pruning of my character came through all these struggles, and how finally tasting that larger meal had mainly come through struggle, much more than easy joy. In fact, I see now bliss is what often numbs me and allows me to be self-reliant, while struggle thrusts me to the feet of Jesus. It seems to be the human condition. Things don't change, like the Israelites in the wilderness who complain about the manna and go make golden calves when struggle is finally removed.[5] I am one of them. We all are.

---

5   *Exodus 16 & 32*

57

How can I live moment by moment clinging to the Vine, in bliss *and* in struggle? I'm still learning this daily and even hourly, clinging and surrendering.

CHAPTER 4

WITH ME IN THE UNKNOWN

You've brought me here to rest
And given me space to breathe
So, I'll stay until it
Sinks in.

Capital City Music
"Lean Back"

I discovered this place a few years before the cancer journey began. Scott and I were struggling to find our bearings in the aftermath of the move, which had left our life and marriage feeling wobbly. I sat in a church pew, not knowing what to do with this heart of mine that was exceeding its capacity to keep everything neatly contained.

The pastor preached through Esther's life, which was marked by her obedience in simply doing the next thing she was supposed to do and leaving the results to God. The job put in front of her was to host the king for dinner, twice. It was God who brought the sleepless night to the king so he could remember her uncle who had saved his life. God was the hinge to the change, not Esther.[6] I realized midway through the sermon that I was trying to be the hinge in our family and our marriage. I wasn't sure if I should stay after the service and ask for prayer or go find a place to be alone with God.

I whispered a quick prayer, "Where do you want me to go? What do I do?"

"Come be with me," is what popped into my head. So, I took that as my divine answer.

I had an hour before I needed to pick up my youngest, so I drove to the ocean cliffs nearby and found a bench at the edge with an unobstructed view of the water.

It was inspiring, beautiful, and peaceful. I wandered over to an empty bench at the edge of the cliff, sat down, and breathed deeply. The ocean is my favorite place in the world. I soaked in the view for a few minutes and let the setting wash over me. Needing some holy therapy, I began writing out my heart on journal pages (instead of just my usual scattered notes from an inspiring book or speaker) and my thoughts and feelings wound their way in and out of written prayers. The pages beckoned me toward honesty and vulnerability which didn't come naturally. But the Lord had been using mentors to nudge me toward a more truthful relationship with God. On

---

6 Esther 6

this bench, I began to let Him pull me into the heart work I so needed.

I followed in the direction I felt led—into some raw confessions, writing them down in black and white and facing them, and letting them face me. Admissions flowed about pride in my own life creeping in subtly behind good intentions of wanting to fix hurt and disappointment in my husband, my broken family, and our hurting world. I'd always wanted to be the hero who brings clarity and heart medicine to others. But God was gently asking me to take off my ill-fitting cape and let Him rightfully wear it instead.

Esther had the king over for dinner; that's all that was asked of her. I could see how I needed to change my story, by seeing myself in her story. My divine Counselor was showing me a path forward, and I was finally learning to listen. I had to let God Himself be the hinge of change as he turned circumstance toward hope. Instead of rushing in with the fix, or answers, or cheerleading, I needed to lean back humbly, and learn to wait for change to come. This was the act of obedience required of me.

After tears of pain and disappointment poured out of my eyes on that bench, I ended with a prayer, "I am excited to see how waiting on your healing—your orchestrating—plays out in this story of our destiny." It felt appropriately significant, maybe even a touch dramatic, but the setting seemed to call for it. And just then, a verse sprang to mind about our words not being wise or persuasive, and faith coming not from human wisdom, but "from God's spirit and power." I was looking for heart healing and wanting to be truly *fathered* by God. I wrote it all down and, seeing the immediate freedom for my heart, I wanted to keep showing up for more. Healing was coming for *me*, while I thought I was bringing it to others! It wasn't a duty or checkbox this time, but a practice of seeking and finding freedom and love.

That day began my sacred meetings with God on the bench.

Two years before finding the bench, we had given up our predictable comfortable life to follow where we thought we saw God leading us. The obedience had led us straight into a wilderness and we questioned everything. For the first time in our twelve years of marriage, we were on different journeys with God. Before the move, we had all our bases covered—the careers, the community, and the house newly renovated down to the last oil-rubbed bronze knob. The pressing sound of God's voice leading us to leave it all behind and follow Him was a surprise. And nearly a year in, jarring disappointment had begun messing with us.

Here we'd chosen surrender and ruthless trust, launched out and left home, but somehow, we were left with a chasm that had grown between us. Discontentment and disconnection were tangling with our old childhood wounds and some mixed-up theology about obedience leading to *blessing*. My cheerleading of Scott's heart wasn't working, nor were his steadfast assurances applying balm to my own soul. By the time I made my way to the bench on the cliffs, I was depleted and thirsting to find God.

I've long been taught that whatever we attempt to quench our thirst with will change the trajectory of our lives, eternally. I technically knew satisfying that thirst with approval, success, productivity, or busyness, always leaves us thirsting for more. But going to God as the true *Well*, finding Him—really finding him—and drinking from Him needed to become more than a good idea. He wanted me to taste and see for myself. It wasn't what I was expecting; it was far greater. I thought I might just gain a better perspective or calmness, but what I found was the realness of God to fill my deepest longings. It feels so personal and almost too precious to share, and part of me wants to keep it close. But a greater part wants to shout it out so everyone can know this amazing gift is real—my daughters, my friends, my family, those who don't know God, yet. His realness. His *with-ness*.

There were so many weights and worries I took to that bench during this journey of wandering in the wilderness. He showed up every time. I began craving it. Sometimes I would come and the anticipation of being with Him felt like I was going out on a first date with all the butterflies and excitement. Other days I would run there like I was starving for my next meal.

My history with this bench and the God who has met me here countless times feels long and true. But it wasn't always confidence that drew me, rather desperation. In weakness and fragility, with an internal quivering that can't be covered up by being outwardly controlled or cheerful or hopeful. This was the place I knew I could be real, my truest self, let it all be exposed, not holding back or keeping it all together, and still leave feeling more loved than when I came. Like going to my divine therapist, my heart always felt more healed after these times of honest vulnerability with God. This was the birthing of really seeing my need for counsel from God, and counsel from wise therapists who could discern, "The purposes of a person's heart are deep waters, [as] one who has insight draws them out."[7]

Like any newer friendship, getting past the acquaintance phase is the only way toward, not just vulnerability, but also amazing depth. I didn't know I was craving this depth with God or even missing it until I tasted it. This experience of prayer being more about listening than talking was so new to me. Prayer had been a checklist of things to cover before, but now it was an amazing conversation with Someone listening and responding in the moment with love that is personal, intentional, and overwhelming. And it's only after all the time I spent on that bench, I can confirm He really does know and love in the most deep and personal way that fills the ache in my soul for realest and purest of love.

One day early into my time at the bench, I'd been soaking in the beauty of the ocean below when I recalled my husband Scott's story. Scott had been at a retreat a few years before where they were encouraged to seek a time of solitude and listening prayer, and to ask God for the name He has for each of them. New names were given to people by God often in the Bible, but does He really still do this today? While Scott sat on a tree stump

7   *Proverbs 20:5 NIV*

64

in the forest of Colorado, God spoke a new name over him. That was amazing and wonderful for Scott, but I was scared to ask God if He had a name for me, scared to not hear something. So, I didn't ask. I had no idea what I would even want my new name to be, as if somehow, I believed God needed some help and input on the matter. How could I know what He would say unless I asked?

I finally got brave enough to ask. I wrote down and whispered the question in my heart to Him. I sat still and looked out over the vast blue waters, the white-capped waves, and surfers riding them. His tender whisper came back to my heart and mind like a gentle breeze blowing: *Delight.*

My breath caught and tears welled up.

Did I hear that right? Show me more so I know for sure this is from You.

I couldn't believe He had actually whispered a name, *my* name and I was reluctant to receive it. Then I opened a book I brought with me that day. The first words I read were a verse printed at the beginning of the chapter:

"The Lord your God is with you; He is mighty to save. He will take great delight in you, He will quiet you with His love, He will rejoice over you with singing."[8]

I am watery-eyed every time I think of it, even as I write this. Seeing it there, written down before me right after I heard it whispered to my heart, I still can hardly believe I'm not making it up. This is how it all went down that day on that sacred ocean bench. I am just one person who gets to tell a love story of God. He writes the best

---

8   *Zephaniah 3:17*

love stories. Like this one He's writing in me now. Immediately, it made me wonder: *How many more divine gifts have I missed by not asking?*

Let me ask you, can you go about your regular day, not feeling so regular in your heart when you've just seen a burning bush. Regular life and life with God are meant to be a fusion, not a separation. I don't have to stay on the bench, or go to a church, or find a monastery (not that I wouldn't love to go to one), or even attend a Bible study to live connected to the Vine. All of those spiritual places and pursuits have been part of my waking up, it's true. But the sweetest times are often the unexpected moments my eyes open, and I sense so clearly that gentle whisper in my heart.

REGULAR LIFE AND LIFE WITH GOD ARE MEANT TO BE A FUSION, NOT A SEPARATION.

This life *with* God and Him with me, is what I am so excited to finally be learning, that His voice is there when I am still and when I seek it. This quiet, calm place in me is where I'm just now beginning to hear His voice.

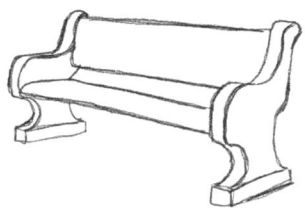

CHAPTER 5

WITH ME IN LIFE AND DEATH

With your final heartbeat,
Kiss the world goodbye.
And go in peace and
laugh on glory's side.

And fly to Jesus
Fly to Jesus
Fly to Jesus and live."

Chris Rice
"Untitled Hymn (Come to Jesus)"

With many sweet encounters on the bench, almost exactly a year after He gave me a new name, I am at that seaside altar again. I've been showing up here as often as I can. It's the place that has become my soul therapy with Jesus, the realest place I can be.

The day before my first thyroid cancer surgery, desperation brings me back. My insides feel uncertain and ominous, but outside it's crystal clear, full of bright sunshine, as are most days living in Southern California. I knew I would find Him here, and I really need a Father-daughter date today where He tells me everything will be okay, and He has it all taken care of. I need Him to look me in the eyes and offer a heart-to-heart pep talk. My own kindhearted Dad died suddenly six years ago, and I really need a dad at this moment.

I was one of those lucky girls who grew up with a dad who adored her. He always made me feel like he would make sure everything was okay. The mayor-like man that everyone knew and loved was jolly, kind, and generous—always quick to treat someone to a latte or a round of golf. He took his role as a provider seriously—and not just with his own family. He once bought a car for one of my first boyfriends.

After my parents' divorce, we started having more heart-level conversations; and, we talked almost every day. He had a way of making me believe I could do anything in life that I set my heart on, and I remember him telling a cashier at a store one time that I was going to be in the Olympics for gymnastics someday. I wasn't even close—ever—to qualifying for that level of competition, but knowing he believed in me as a young girl was a rich treasure. Hearing him tell others of his confidence in me made my young heart bloom.

His dark side later surfaced when I learned he was skilled at compartmentalizing his convictions. He began making choices that could no longer be hidden. In my twenties, I found out I had a little baby half-sister on the way. That conversation was full of hurt and disappointment, and I needed every bit of the lead-up time to her birth to process the news and prepare my heart to lovingly receive my sister. A few months after the news came another wedding, and a few years later, another divorce. Dad had finally hit the bottom of trying to hide the struggle, and we entered the broken, beautiful place where he began turning back to God in a real way.

The day before he died, we had all been together at my grandfather's funeral, of all things, on my mom's side. Dad seemed unusually tired and more burdened than I'd expected. I called him later that evening to tell him that his grandson, my nephew, had his heart stirred at the funeral and said he wanted to commit his life to God. We celebrated over the phone and said goodnight and goodbye with full hearts. The next afternoon he called to let me know that he had had the winning putt to qualify for his dream golf tournament at Pebble Beach the next month. It was the last time I would hear his voice, and after we hung up, he took a nap from which he never awoke. The call came a few hours later from a friend who found him *asleep* at his house, and paramedics were unable to revive him. He died in his sleep. It shattered my heart with the deepest ache I had ever known. I fell to my knees and wept.

Growing darkness overwhelmed both the sky and my soul as we made the long drive down to the hospital to confirm his identity and say goodbye to his shell. In the quiet, unable to soak in the shock, God whispered to my heart sweet memories one after the other. My mind was so disoriented, I wasn't able to process thoughts, but they kept reeling one after the other.

The waiting room was full of people. They seemed fuzzy as I numbly walked in for my final moments with one of my favorite people on this earth. He was covered in a white sheet and had freshly cut grass on his socks and a smile on his face. He was finally free of the burdens and hurts he carried. I thought about how he was leaving this earth on a perfect day for him, but way too early for me. My now seven-year-old half-sister would never know her dad the way I had known him.

Death definitely had its sting that day and in the days to come. My lightheartedness was snuffed out. I felt heavy, unsure I was strong enough to carry this deep pain: so much to sort through, to decide, to discern, to grieve. His service was five days later on St. Patrick's Day. The church was packed. Our old Cleaver life merged with our newly fragmented family life, and we all grieved together as he passed into the presence of Jesus. My tears fell heavy and hard.

Even the baristas at his Starbucks sent flowers and cards saying they would miss making his Skinny Vanilla Latte. The bagpiper played Amazing Grace in front of his casket and at his tomb site on that overcast, drizzly day. It was holy and beautiful. The reception was appropriately at the golf course country club, just as he would've wanted. I still have the winning ball he played on his last earthly day—even took it with me to St Andrews in Scotland later that fall.

I sought out these little wins and celebrations of him that made my heart come up for air—especially that he had turned back to a real pursuit of God before he went to meet Him in person. God really does bring beauty from ashes. Then, nine months after his sudden death, our surprise little gift of life and joy, Natalie, our youngest daughter, came into our world. A few months before her arrival, we were sifting through all my dad's things, and I found his old Bible which he had used for thirty years. In his own writing he had written a girl name and a boy name with their meanings. We had already found out we were expecting a girl and decided on her name. The girl's name written by the hand of my dad, was Natalie, "gift of joy." Not sure how to reason my way through this *coincidence* but I soaked it in as a gift—a gift from God to my hurting heart reminding me He was with me in life and death and a gift to her from her Grandpa Skip, whom she will only meet in eternity.

As a young mom, suddenly fatherless, I was comforted reading through the Psalms, being reminded of how God is a Father to the fatherless. I wasn't sure what I needed; I just knew I missed him, and so God brought himself and Godfathered my heart. He brought us family-we-choose, to be dads and mentors in our lives, with room in their hearts for ours. I wasn't seeking it; He just brought them. I saw it was Him intentionally leading their hearts toward us.

Still today on this bench, He is fathering me with whispers that touch my aching, deep need for fatherly comfort. I remember the repetition three times: *I am with you, I am with you, I am with you.* That was the kind of fathering my heart needed most. I see this now as the *with-God life* that He brings, beyond anything I think or imagine—even in death.

Heart-fixing was promised in those whispers at the ocean alter. I'm learning the gift of hearing God. I'm learning to thirst for Him at the well. I'm learning to be still, listen, and breathe.

Seeing where words and the Person whispering the word merge, and I realize how words are more important than I ever supposed. Saying, "I believe," in these personal words whispered to my heart, and in the Person whispering them, makes the difference between life and death. "For Jesus doesn't impose salvation as a solution, He narrates salvation into being through leisurely conversation, intimate personal relationships, compassionate responses, passionate prayer, and -putting it all together-a sacrificial death. We don't casually walk away from words like that."[9]

I only came for comfort, but at this crossroads of life and death, He's narrating my own salvation on this very bench. I'm invited to freshly grieve this most difficult death. Our souls and His words are the only things that really will last forever. His presence is bringing real life to my hurting heart, here and now, on this side of eternity.

---

9   *Eugene Peterson, "The Daily Message" (NavPress, Colorado Springs, CO, 2005), p.1570.*

Remembering my dad and how I was fathered by God was the preparation I needed for what is to come. He's prepared me today, as He has been all along, for the resilience I will require in the months to come. This is my ongoing discovery as my days at the bench swell. This Good Father knows I need the preparation, comfort, and connection to Him; and, this is where I know I can find Him.

CHAPTER 6

WITH ME IN EMPTINESS

When I'm on fire when
You're near me
I'm on fire, when You speak
And I'm on fire,
Burning at these mysteries,
These mysteries…

Switchfoot
"On Fire"

Getting to the other side of the cancer sprint, and now jumping back into our regular full-filled life, makes me feel unsteady. Regular scans, healing scars, and new job opportunities intersect as we pack moving boxes. We're moving our family up to Northern California. Three short months on the other side of this whirlwind body-and-soul journey, we are on a new one, out of the wilderness in which we'd found ourselves. We are returning to the place we left three years prior, though that ocean bench will always be a piece of home. Since we can't make the moving company load up the bench with us, Scott in his loving way has a professional take a photo of the sacred bench and mount it on canvas for

LIFE HAS A WAY OF PRESSING FORWARD, EVEN WHEN WE ARE NOT READY FOR IT.

our new home five hundred miles away. Our life together is an *area under restoration*, like the signs we saw along the shore where new growth was being tended.

Life has a way of pressing forward, even when we are not ready for it. I just want to stay here in this space and not forget, keep learning to live more fully than I did before. Before we can blink, we are back in full swing. That tender, more alive space is hard to hold onto and can feel fleeting. Soon, a full year flies by with a new house, new school, new church, new jobs, new benches, and new blood tests and body scans. We've left behind a kind of wilderness yet remain unsure what lies ahead.

As we sort out and try to make sense of the pieces and fragments of that three-year stint, we find we're grieving a dream we thought would bring more purpose and meaning to our lives. We'd dreamed of working outside of corporate America and hoped trading it for a more dependent, trusting-on-God sort of place would bring purpose, along with *blessing*; but, it hadn't. This broken dream left us with neck scars and heart wounds we needed mended.

For the next several months, once a week we sit on the couch of a gifted wise counselor, who affirms our need for understanding. Our mixed-up theology of the *blessed life* apparently got tangled up in our old stories, and we're relearning that the blessing is the *with-God life*— not the storm-free or comfortable life. There's no way to shortcut a very complicated deconstruction process we have to work on and through for these months. We have so much sorting out to do together and with God.

I think of the disciples on the boat out in the torrential storm—Jesus with them—and they're still freaking out. They ask in a panic, "Don't you care if we drown?" How quick they were to doubt His intentions for them.[10] He calms the storm and reminds them not to be afraid. I need this reminder too. Storms will come. He brings calm in them. Scott and I need God to break our American ideas of blessing without suffering, and remind us again of His true, faithful presence in the storms—He really is the *with us* God. Apparently, I need to be told three times (or more) that He is with me before it sinks down as a truth I anchor to my heart. More storms are on the horizon.

The one-year checkup of labs and scans shocks the doctors and rocks my world again. It is back. It has spread. My "happy face" scar needs a major expansion from two inches to an unbelievable ten. The storm has whipped up again. Although this time around, I am

---

10   *Mark 4:38*

mostly still believing He is with me in the good and the not-so-good.

Despite what I know in my head about God's trustworthiness, this really feels not good. I plop myself under that canvas picture of the bench thinking about the new scars I will have by this time tomorrow. I struggle with laying down fears that threaten to pull me under. Surrendering, breathing deep, trying to remember—it's all I can do. Light shines in through the window touching the bench on the canvas, and I see His light. I sense the soul-balm and my fears lighten. Wonderfully, just moments after my little freak-out, my dear friend who walked closely with me the first time through calls to check in. I lose all composure telling her the news.

My fears are about many things: complications of surgery, questions of whether it will keep coming back again, and how I will feel with the withdrawal of thyroid medications. Then there are the hearts of my little daughters who are now a year older and more aware and asking questions of their own. And I am really not ready and willing to be so needy again. I wanted this sprint to be done. I'd given it everything I had the last time and worried I had nothing left in the tank. How quickly my utter dependence on Him had moved back to my old self-reliance.

How do I stay in this space with Him? I run to be with God in a quiet place in the house and wait for His whisper to come. *I need the bench. No,* I think, *I really just need Him.* I remind myself and remember that He is way beyond the bench. He is God. The Creator of the

Universe, yet He knows my heart. I lament on the journal pages, ask my questions, and listen. His whisper comes again. I write it down because I need the reminding that tells me He is still with me. I am not alone. I can trust Him for healing. He "tends to His flock like a shepherd, gathers his lambs in His arms close to His heart, and gently leads those that have young."[11] I have young. I am young. I need Him. There is that uncomfortable, but necessary, neediness again. Yes, being close to Him is what I need most!

I am not good at knowing what my needs are or giving them attention. I try explaining to Scott what I think I need; and, he gently says words I need to hear.

"Sweetie, you are a hard person to help."

A pang of guilt. I gulp. I don't want to be that way. I want to learn the humility of receiving, but it is so hard.

I enjoy being the giver so much, but God is at work in my heart and getting me to a true point of need. So, I am learning to ask, instead of waiting to be asked. I am learning that the one who knows my most intimate needs is our great God who supplies through His presence and His people who He sends.

Project *happy-face expansion* gets underway, with my Divine Surgeon and Chief Branch Pruner. Once again, I find myself at my new employer not as nurse, but as patient. I want so badly to be the one standing at the gurney helping again, instead of the one being helped. But I surrender, put on the homemade colorful gown from my nurse friend, smile with my skillful surgeon for

11   *Isaiah 40:11 ESV*

the photo, bring treats again for all my caretakers, and head off to Never-Never-Land with my lulling anesthesia.

I wake up to a new scar across the front and now also the side of my neck, a drain in my chest, sharp pains, and 29 fewer lymph nodes. This time there is just skin glue and no bandage to hide this pruning. I wake up in recovery and see the faces of my best friends from college who flew in to be at my bedside, and a waiting room full this time for me, for Scott, for our family. Learning to let others into the struggle helps carry our burdens instead of being burdens. Humility and surrender are in the gift of receiving. Our girls come to visit and the looks on their faces show they are not thinking it looks like a happy face anymore. This time we share the cancer word with them and let them begin walking through their own journeys of struggle with questions for God, while holding them close.

LEARNING TO LET OTHERS INTO THE STRUGGLE HELPS CARRY OUR BURDENS INSTEAD OF BEING BURDENS.

The diet and the body prep start again. All too familiar. It's Mother's Day. Scott and the girls spoil me with a low-iodine breakfast in bed and later, lunch served on the couch where I am trying to lay in those green pastures David writes about in the Psalms. I'm able to pull up strength to go to church and enjoy worshiping God, but am unable to hold back tears when I feel His Spirit moving. He is with me, so very close. Struggle and suffering are met with the gift of His *with-ness* is the *eternity-now* place I want to stay in.

During the next weeks on the journey to thyroid emptiness, my body feels out of fuel with no medications to counteract the side effects of a not having a thyroid. My body feels like it's a thousand pounds and even the small things feel like so much effort. I live somewhere between my chronically tired college days and the kind of head fogginess I imagine comes with aging. My surgeon tries to prepare me for the weakness, aching, exhaustion, emotions, and the sedated feeling that everything is moving at half speed. A week into my low-iodine diet, I am adjusting and trying to remember to use the optimistic wisdom my parents taught me growing up—to look at what I can eat/have/do, not what I can't. And oh, how that changes my attitude! Thanks, Mom.

We go to church on Sunday and hear the president of Compassion International talk about the plague of childhood hunger in the world. All of a sudden, I'm thankful for my light and momentary hunger that is more a result of unmet cravings than actual lack of food. I say goodbye to chocolate chip cookies and coffee with cream, and hello to many other choices. The joy that comes in discovering Trader Joe's coconut milk without dairy, salt, or soy, and is also low iodine feels like Christmas morning.

In God's perfect timing, when I open the pages of my Bible-in-a-Year, I read the words of the mountain sermon from the lips of Jesus,

"You're blessed when you are at the end of your rope. With less of you there is more of God.... You're blessed when you've worked up a good appetite for God.

He's food and drink in the best meal you'll ever have... You're blessed when you care. At the moment of being 'care-full' you find yourself cared for..." [amen to that] *"Steep your life in God-reality, God-initiative, God-provisions... Give your entire attention to what God is doing right now, and don't get worked up about what may or may not happen tomorrow. God will help you deal with whatever hard things come up when the time comes."* [12]

His Divine mending comes again with the most fitting and timeless words that make my glass feel half full instead of half empty (with low-iodine coconut milk).

Tomorrow marks the start of my God time *isolation* retreat, round two. We squeeze in a family game of UNO, root beer, and Snickers bars—our family vacation tradition—even though I have to pass on the Snickers. It's the final moment of normalcy before the scans and double dose of nuclear run-off. I will head to a beautiful local guest house about five minutes from ours. Instead of an ocean view this year, it looks out across three acres of oak trees. My hosts are strangers who invited me in, a radioactive-contaminated sick guest. I am so moved that

---

12   Peterson, *"The Daily Message,"* p. 446.

God provided such a perfect place to heal, to rest; and, I know He is already there to welcome me.

The Lord sends in the troops to help this needy soldier in the form of family and friends who are in the fox hole with me, while I go *James Bond dark* for five days. Even though I will not have any visitors until I return home, this time I know I will not be alone.

Wondering if the radiating glow can be seen over my cottage in the woods, I settle into my not-so-isolated time with a stock of low-iodine food, clothes, books, and my empty body. It is a good morning here in my little hideaway as I watch the sun come up, listen to the birds sing, and cling to the ability to taste the good French press coffee, cream-free. When I had asked the nuclear medicine doctor (who had a great sense of humor, geek-squad style) if I could take a picture of the lead-lined canister with my *nuclear run-off* pill inside, he said, "Of course. And, let me put the Geiger counter next to it since I will be using that on you next." It really did feel like a scene of 007 when it started beeping like crazy as he pointed it at my scarred neck.

This medicine blows me away at how effective and unique it is. The radiation only kills thyroid cells, not other healthy cells like in traditional chemotherapy. If they had this intervention for all cancer types, it would be revolutionary. The doctor said my thyroid tank was not just on fumes or even empty. It was so vacated that he described it as having "cobwebs." This means I can start taking a double dose of thyroid medication a few days from now. Oh, happy day! It is like being told I can have water again after a seven-year drought.

What are my plans today at my cottage in the woods? Simplicity, solitude, rest, reading, listening to music and nature, being still, drinking lots of water, soaking up His Living Water, healing, praying, journaling, burning candles, peeing out this radiation, and flipping through my new Sunset magazine.

The *with me* God really does show up for me here like I hoped He would, and even beyond what I hoped. The radiation peaks at about 24 hours, like clockwork. The first few days are the toughest with intense nausea, a stiff and sore neck, unquenchable thirst, body aches, and weakness. Lying still on the bed is all I can do. Reading or journaling requires energy I don't have, so I just lie here and turn on music. In this moment of laying flat on my back in stillness, I can almost feel the hand of God rub my head like a dad sitting beside my hospital bed.

Wanting to pray, but too weak even for that, I turn the iPad on Genius play to automatically choose amongst my hundreds of songs. My head is so foggy I can't even pick a playlist. A song starts that I can honestly say I have no recollection of hearing before. Perhaps a song I forgot about, but it feels like God answering prayers I can't even utter, as nuclear tears roll down my cheeks. If I could have prayed, the lyrics and passion in them are *exactly* what I feel. I can't get over it. If I could have journaled my prayer, it would have been these very words, "Thirsting to need filling, strength, and healing for the journey is long…"[13]

I put the song on repeat, listening, absorbing, crying, and receiving the gift He's giving me. It is so *God*, so overwhelmingly perfect. I glance over at the iPad Genius, knowing it really is divine genius, and I take note of the song. Don Poythress? Never heard of him or this song. God is rejoicing over me with singing like the Good Book says. It's like He told the DJ to play this song for me, just to let me feel His love, His care, His healing. I drift off to sleep while it plays. This is grace. Not from my doing but a gift from Him.

I wake early at the cottage and sit on the back porch with the sunlight filtering through the oak trees, sipping coffee, singing "Waiting Here for You," and reading words of God shining more of His Light on this journey with His timeless megaphone again,

> "What we've learned is this, that God does not respond to what we do, we respond to what God does... Sheer gift... we throw open the doors to God and discover at the same moment He has already thrown open His door to us... we know how troubles can develop passionate patience in us, and how that patience in turn forges the tempered steel of virtue, keeping us alert for what God will do next... we can't round up enough

---

13   *Don Poythress & Jared Anderson, "Fill Me Up," Wash Away (2009).*

> containers to hold everything God
> generously pours into our lives through
> the Holy Spirit!"[14]

It started out feeling like an eternity, but in no time homecoming arrives, and I am giddy. While it has been a soul-filling retreat in so many ways, there really is no place like home. The thought of hugging Scott and the girls makes my heart leap. The day before, I did get a sneak peek at them when they dropped off a high-iodine In-N-Out burger and a shake. They had some sad moments of missing mom over the past few days, but were able to work through them with phone calls, distance hugs, good talks and singing to sleep on speaker phone, and lots of extra Daddy love. My knight-in-shining-armor has been just that and has truly been loving me through better or worse, in sickness and health. I am so blessed to have his strength and tenderness.

After getting packed up, cleaned up, geared up for my finish line sprint, I sit on the couch in the cottage wanting one more encounter with Jesus before I leave this sacred space. It is quiet and still. I turn on the Genius playlist and open the same book I read at my first radioactive retreat a year ago, the one on the power of gratitude in struggle. I open to chapter 10, and the title of the chapter is, "Empty to Fill." My notes written in my own hand, from the ocean bench six months before, are from Him:

"I will fill you...."

---

14   Peterson, "The Daily Message," p.535.

and my response is

"I love how you fill me, God."

How did He know? And, how am I just now seeing it? I start writing my heart on pages with tears streaming. Then the Genius starts playing song after song that have been gifts to me on this journey of struggle and emptiness. As the next song plays, each one has a new meaning and feels to me like new knowing and deeper loving. I can't believe it. I start writing down the order of the songs, not wanting to forget any details of this gift:

> "Healer" – My theme song since my first retreat.
>
> "I Surrender All" – My Dad's favorite hymn.
>
> "Tis' so sweet to trust in Jesus" – My favorite hymn.
>
> "Grace" – "It shines on me."
> "I'm nothing without You" and "everything in You."
>
> "Broken and Beautiful" – "We remember," "this is the way You make all things new," "extravagant love," "prodigal grace, mercy's embrace."

"I Love to Praise Your Name" – My favorite instrumental piece that I frequently played on the bench.

"I Belong" – "Nothing can take me from your great love," "I belong to You, forever this truth remains."

"Here is Love" – "Vast as the ocean," "grace and love like mighty rivers," "your love is higher, wider, deeper, truer," "it's your love."

I am no longer depleted, but truly filled—feeling I've been danced with and sung over by the most personal, knowing, and loving God. "I can't absorb or take any more of your Presence," I whisper, "Like Moses only able to see the back of You. Can you please end this precious time with the song you sang over me my first night here?"

I believe, I believe. And yes, He does. The next song to play is, "Fill Me Up."

"Spirit come, Fill up my lungs with air, my voice with prayer

And my mouth with praise

Fill up my heart with songs for the journey is long

And I need your cleansing…

You are water to the desert,

You are the rain to the dust,

You are healing to the broken,

You are life…

I need your strength, Your love is more
than enough,

Come and fill me up."[15]

I'm pretty sure I just had *The Shack* experience at the country cottage. All I can say is He is real and personal. We can experience Him on this side of Heaven. He wooed my heart to fall completely into His love.

I am discharged from my second round of isolation with renewed soul strength, even in my weak body state—renewed in who He is and believing that He really is a *with me* God, that trusting does not always bring clarity, but gratefulness brings trusting, that emptiness is the best place to get filled with Him, that benches, and hospitals, hotel rooms, and country cottages can all be a sanctuary to meet Him, that if I seek Him, I will find Him.

Even when life starts getting back to the wonderfully *normal* I've craved, I don't want to let this new etching on my heart get dulled. I want Him to fill me up with more of Him. My new bigger happy face on my neck will be a daily reminder. An altar of remembrance on my body, which will fade but never go away. Like the scars on His hands for me.

---

15   Poythress & Anderson, "Fill Me Up."

I officially cross the finish line of this physical, emotional, and spiritual race. I have that, "Whoa-what-just-happened?" feeling for days and sponging up all the amazing goodness from the journey is on my new to-do list.

The day after I officially lose all taste from the radiation effects, I read the words of David reminding me to, "taste and see that the Lord is good."[16] He really does have a sense of humor and is so funny with timing and words, isn't He? Just as my tastebuds get a shot of general anesthesia, my sense of smell and my mind can still enjoy all the iodine goodness. I try to wake them back up by gorging on about 20 pieces of saltwater taffy, hoping to hyper-salivate them out of their slumbering state. After two months I kind of start to taste again, but I'm definitely tasting the goodness of God and continuing to find soul rest in Him.

A few weeks after my experience at *The Shack*, I go in for my final body scan. All clear. So now we put on the cruise control and enjoy the sights on the other side of the journey. But, I am tasting and seeing in new ways now. And, I never want to forget again.

---

16   *Psalm 34:8*

CHAPTER 7

A DAILY SALVATION EXPERIENCE

If faith can move the mountains
Let the mountains move
We come with expectation
Waiting here for you.

Christy Nockles
"Waiting Here for You"

A year of good news marches on, and I find myself at a Passionist Retreat Center[17] on the one-year anniversary of my latest homecoming. Our godparents introduced us to this sacred place—a place for rest and renewal. In this new season, I'm learning the importance

---

17   *There are 10 Passionist Centers throughout the US, available for rest, renewal, and weekend retreats. Find out more at passionist.org.)*

of making room for being reminded. So much rejoicing and reviving is found in remembering the journey.

While I'm here, breathing in the stillness and gift of life, my heart becomes burdened for others to experience this realness and sweet friendship of Jesus whether on a bench, in a cottage, or in everyday moments—not with any *shoulds* or *checklists*, just the life-giving stuff from the Life-Giver. I don't know what it completely means yet, but my heart is enraptured by the idea of getting more involved in some way, helping those I feel God misses most, and those who miss His sweet pursuit.

Cancer is an equalizer, one that touches all of us in some way. While it's opened my eyes to appreciate my health and the time I have, it's also become a thorn in my side threatening to steal, kill, and destroy my joy in living fully alive. Living the moments and days without fear of cancer, uncertainty, doubt, or wondering is a daily struggle of surrender. I feel as if I'm waiting for cancer to show up again. I don't like it. Waiting is tough. So I begin attempting to more regularly renew my mind with truth from God's Word.

Through this struggle of waiting and surrender, I begin finding the truth again, that long-awaited true life, and I try to recover my way to live with a free heart. He reminds me to be still on my bench, to keep my eyes fixed on Him, not on the waves. I find the wind and waves still really do listen to Him. I remember how this was much easier to believe and actually practice when sitting at my oceanfront altar, than in the day-to-day moments of struggle.

Are we ever really done with struggle? Why is there never a point of completion? He gently reminds me there is more struggle ahead, and I wish we could just go back to hearing the part about His love. But reluctantly, He's teaching me that both parts—the struggle and the love—are essential to knowing the full blessing. It just looks so different than my earlier concept of blessing, that ideal of an *American blessing*. I'm finding God's blessing is much more about never leaving me alone in the struggle. I'm reminded struggles, pain, heartbreak, cancer, they are all part of this broken life as we march on. But the *with-God life* keeps my heart freer on the journey. In these moments, I sense the eternity placed in all of our hearts, my longing for Eden again, struggle-free, hurt-free, and burden-free. My heart hears this, and I write it down:

"Look and listen for My power to lift you up, not your own. Be still with me; I am the One who brings Peace. Keep your focus on Me, my Delight. I still have plans for your life that I will unfold in My time. But watch and listen; you will find Me in it. It is My Glory I want to shine through you in all I ask of you. I am WITH you always."

There it is again, that reminder of *with*, the theme He wants me to really believe and live. To share this "Gift of With" story transforms duty into a beautiful love story.

Writing these sacred soul words down still makes my heart quiver in knowing that the God of the Universe really knows and sees and cares about the details of all of us. How He knows and loves so personally and intimately blows my mind, and I try to absorb it at my deepest core. When I do, I taste heaven. I long for more, but also with a deep contentment.

Being *with* Him, I wonder why do I live on appetizers, or "bread alone," and miss out on this feast with Him? My stubborn self is starting to get it—I need more of Him. Yes, this is real living now. The expanded happy face scar is starting to fade and is hardly noticed. My heart doesn't want to lose what the scars have taught me. This living the *with-God life* is the good life.

As the months pass with waiting on results, I get an opportunity to go on my first medical mission in the Philippines, to help care for kids with cleft lips and palates, whose broken faces beam with broken, holy smiles. Now I get to help make happy faces on little ones overlooked and ignored. Tossing between my long-time desire to be part of this meaningful adventure, with my fears of the unknown, I find yet another new bench. It overlooks a pond instead of an ocean. It is shaded by a tree with a small trickle of water falling over its edge and turtles that sunbathe on the overflow wall. God even shows up on ordinary benches in regular neighborhoods. I sit and soak in the quiet and ask God if this mission trip is from Him. I hear, "Go, I will be with you and take care of you." There it is again, *with*. So, I say, "Yes," after asking for more confirmation, of course. I think I understand Gideon from the Bible story with the fleece.[18] Benches are becoming my sanctuary, my hospital bed, and my therapy couch where I hold out my fleeces in trembling hands and wait for His response.

Then, just two days before I leave on this new adventure, I get some new dreaded lab results. It is back. Round 3. The waves come for me again, swirling and tossing; like Peter, my feet start to sink. I don't want this. Not again. I plead for Jesus to take me back to the boat with Him, and my heart is sinking fast. Do I still go on this trip? I feel as though I should stay and figure out what is next, or maybe just hunker down and try to manage what I can control. I remember His "go" and "with" words from the bench, and so I stick to the plan and go anyway, leave my family and friends, and taking with me a ruthless, defiant trust. Whatever comes, I will be with Him and He with me. This was what I needed to get my eyes off of my waves. Serving others brings the needed heart transformation and new perspective. This was the medicine I truly needed, my RX: *surrender.*

Seeing hundreds of kids with mangled smiles in the arms of their worn-out mommas makes my scars feel beautiful and small. Eating mostly rice at every meal reminds me of the low-iodine diet, yet I don't have hunger pains like they do. The pangs of cancer start to fade and lose their grip as I get to be a nurse to the

---

18   *Judges 6:36-39*

forgotten and afflicted children a half a world away. When I pray for healing, He brings it, healing to my self-absorbed heart. I take my Catholic prayer candle and burn it all night in my hotel room to remind me of the quiet steady presence of God with me on this trip and will be with me on this Round-3 battle with my greatest enemy. I hang onto the words He has whispered to my heart.

I've found space for my inner healing through serving and through time and stillness with God again. He lifts me up with His presence, and I feel renewed, but not by my own strength or determination. The only thing I need to *do* is open the door of my heart and invite Him in, often, daily, hourly. I'm learning that I don't have to wait for eternity to experience the realness of God with me. I get it now. When I leave room for Him, and let Him come, He gives me more of Him.

On my last day, I open the pages of my Bible and read, "And remember your journey... to know the righteous acts of the Lord... act justly, love mercy, and walk humbly with God."[19] I land on home soil with more tenderness for others and more hope in what lies ahead.

This round is full of the dreaded word, *wait*. Waiting rooms, waiting and watching, waiting impatiently, waiting in wonder. How do you live fully in the waiting? I want to rush in and cut it out. The Cancer Board of Doctors meet, review my chart and my history, and they decide to wait and watch to see what is best for this chronic state of cancer I've become. If it grows, the

---

19   *Micah 6:5-8 (NLT)*

happy face will be expanded again. For now, I just have to let this monster keep growing in my body. I'm scared and fatigued by the thought that this will take me out. This feels less like a journey now, certainly not a sprint, but more like an ultra-marathon I never chose to join and can't quit—even though I desperately want to. My doctor tells me that I will most likely have to deal with this every few years now, getting treatment and a new neck-slicing. Just like that.

Yikes. I need a bench.

I let a few weeks pass because it takes me a while to remember, but I finally go to a bench. I bring my worn journals with me. I need reminding and re-counseling in this wait-and-watch therapy. I glance back at those pages and dates, and it's been exactly three years and three days since I was on the ocean bench hearing His whisper three times that He is *with* me. My breath catches and tears come again. This is my third round. He knew then what I am just knowing now. *He knew.* He is in the details and knows the layers of my soul. This is so holy and sacred, I can barely speak it. I can't help but shout out the goodness and amazing love of God. He tenderly shows me from one bench to another that He has been with me, like He said He would. This is His story for me, and for all who let Him come near.

He knows I need to hear things at least three times to get traction in this stubborn heart, to validate that I heard Him, and to remind me He is true. The eyes of my heart see how He has seen me all along. When others try to soothe me with cliches that really only leave me empty,

He fills. I had no idea how empty I would become, and my crowded heart had been squeezing Him out. The promise of those words, "I am with you," flood my very being and I weep my thanks. Healing continues in new ways, yet I walk with the *limp* of wrestling with God, with neck scars to remind me.

In the in-between times, He speaks His care and love over me, reminding me He is with me so closely in this. When I rise and when I sleep, I am not alone. He strengthens me with His hands. When I step toward Him, He draws near to me. He is seemingly always waiting for me to show up, as if He is sitting there just waiting for me, and I begin realizing I move through so much of life with a misunderstanding that I am waiting on Him.

He doesn't just stay on the bench, he comes with us on the journey. Soul waiting is a daily salvation experience. Thoughts, wishes, fears, and hopes are hushed into calm and quiet by the great Peace of His Presence bringing profound transformation. My worry webs lose their grip. Waiting is teaching me absolute dependence on Him, and strength then comes with patient endurance. So I renew my focus on cultivating this habit of waiting for His words beyond the bench. In waiting, dependence, giving, and gratitude, I am brought the peace I need. My heart is the scene of His Divine Operation, and His scars heal mine.

CHAPTER 8

TELLING THE STORY

He set my feet upon a rock,
And made my footsteps firm
Many will see, many will
see and fear…

U2
"40"

My first surgeon gave me early warnings to resist scouring beyond the basic WebMD and Mayo Clinic sites to gather information about my diagnosis. Stick to the evidence-based medicine, he said. I am pretty sure he could tell I am one of those helicoptering, vigilant nurses that like to fix and control, even though I am unaware how tight my fists can become. He was trying to spare me from the darkness of cancer blogs that suck you down instead of lifting you up; I was thankful for his intervention.

Advice comes at me constantly from very caring people. "Eat four cups of asparagus every day," they say. "Drink kombucha. Read this or that homeopathic book, the one with Bible verses cited." I try to remain gracious and thank them, but I know that's not where my help is coming from. I continue to go to my time with God and experience new life, not duty, but simple stillness, listening, conversation time with Him. I find myself not consumed with anxious thoughts of science and statistics, but with peace from His whispered words.

A few months after the third diagnosis, the results are "no change" which means more waiting, but no slicing and dicing on my neck just yet. I rejoice. This is strength training for my eyes and my heart to remain fixed and steady. I feel like I can take a long deep breath. They tell me we can wait until the new masses get to a certain size before we cut them out; this is a new kind of waiting. I'll need more surgery and treatment as the doctors order labs and tests and rechecks every few months—we just don't know when. It seems the chance of total healing is far away. Yet the former dread and anticipation I'd felt is hitting stretches of days, sometimes weeks, without consuming my thoughts. Maybe I'm actually learning something here.

The "renewing of my mind" is the exercise that brings strength, and my mind is the biggest and most stubborn muscle to train in my body. When my mind surrenders to the anxious what-ifs, my heart embraces true peace. Finding that place in the tension, not in denial or resignation, but in a steady surrender and trust is hard work. The lessons cannot be dependent on the cancer outcome or test results, but on really knowing and believing that He is *with* me.

Of course, I still always desire full healing, but I'm trying to hold a steadier gaze on Jesus and not the waves, and it keeps me from tossing or drowning when the seas get rough. I'm reminded of a recent family movie night, and a scene in *The Hobbit* when Bard has to support the heavy metal arrow on his son's shoulder to try and take out the dragon. His son is gripped with fear as the approaching dragon spews flames and death threats. "Look at me, son," the master marksman beckons. "Just look at me." He remains perfectly calm, and it calms his son, too. I hold that picture with me for months, the secret to calm amidst encroaching evil. This is my soul-training to slay my dragons.

Three more months pass in the new waiting practice. I find myself on a bench again for another therapy session with Him. I'm still learning to come here before being desperate and hungry, like a regular appointment, just showing up to create space for more of Him. New results will come tomorrow. I need to be empty of fear and worry, simply full of the peace and love of God.

I try to remember: How do I have peace in the unknowns, the waiting, the fears? I look up. It is simply from Him, through surrender and trust as a daily practice, on benches usually, as I make space and time to seek. Benches are still one of the best places for me to force myself to be still. Just. Be. With. Him. It isn't complicated or overly spiritual. It's pretty simple to seek Him if I can only remember to. Breathing deeply in His name, inviting Him in, and learning to listen is always how I find Him.

It always involves prayer and then some added space to just listen to my heart. I'm reminded these hidden treasures aren't hard to find when I let go of the busyness blocking my soul.

In a few days, the results come in and it is "the same" yet again, which means another three months of waiting—no surgery. I am really starting to pay attention to threes. Fears are transformed into hope by His with-ness and waiting is getting a little easier.

... I REALIZE WAITING IS TEACHING ME ABSOLUTE DEPENDENCE ON HIM THROUGH PATIENT ENDURANCE.

A stronger Pollyanna outlook begins to take over as I realize waiting is teaching me absolute dependence on Him through patient endurance. I ask Jesus to help me be still enough, humble enough, simple enough to be a canvas of His great action and story. I want Him to write the screenplay. I notice it is becoming less effort to fearlessly wait, peaceful whatever the outcome. Like Job who reminds me that taking the good days and the troubled days are part of the blessing. Shifting my worldview to no longer think good is only defined by me, is also a blessing.

Three more months go by. There will be more testing and results coming. Today I am on the banks of a peaceful river, not an ocean bench this time. I sit with Him. His whisper comes to my heart, "I am with you, Janelle, My Delight. I am holding you in My hand. I have a greater purpose in this struggle. It is for My glory. I will show you. Trust Me. Abide. Be humble. Be close to Me. I am here. Listen for Me."

The repeat labs and news of "stability" comes along with the gift of more waiting. Gratitude floods my heart for His mercy, His presence, His care, His story being written in me, His plan, His purpose. I'm finally believing and grasping the truth that God is with me at all times! I'm not sure I can explain what's changed, but it is the most amazing gift and blessing. Something in me believes it and feels it more now. The peace and light it brings refreshes and satisfies my soul like nothing else. He breathes His life into mine, and I'm excited I can continue waiting, watching, and trusting with Him.

The richness and fullness of regular life continues on with the underlying deep streams of peaceful waiting running below my deeper awareness. The events of my life and heart feel deeper than before, though regular life is certainly not epic. It's ordinary: full of packing lunches, taxiing my girls to a million activities, coffee dates with friends, working as a nurse, going on walks after dinner with my husband, leading small groups of little people on their own journey in finding God, and weekly trips to Trader Joe's to stock the refrigerator. But all of it now feels more alive somehow, and I'm consciously aware of the gentle whisper of God.

Why was I thinking God would come in the wind, the fire, the earthquake? Instead, He comes in the everyday and ordinary. But first it was the quiet, still moments, when I could stop; and, He could get my attention. He's in the song, in the beauty of His Creation, and in a grateful heart. And, on the new *benches* I now find He provides wherever I look along the way.

It has now been three sets of three months of waiting. Time passed with no new growing cancer in my body. My bench time has moved to my kitchen table in the early morning hours He continues counseling me on the pages of Matthew's gospel story of Jesus. This very morning, the same God, my Divine Therapist, is teaching me how to live fully alive. This is what I read:

> "... find Him in a quiet secluded place and be simple and honest in prayer, sense His grace. In prayer there is a connection between what He does and what I do... look at the birds, free, unfettered, not tied down... relax... don't be preoccupied with getting, so I can respond to God's giving... steep my life in God-reality, God-initiative, God provisions... give my entire attention to what He is doing right now and don't get worked up about what may or may not happen tomorrow. God will help me deal with whatever hard

things come up when the time comes…
forget about yourself, look to Jesus, and
I find both… get away with Jesus and
I find Life. Walk with Him and work
with Him, watch how He does it. Learn
the unforced rhythms of grace… keep
company with Him and I learn to live
freely and lightly."[20]

This is what I put on the pages of my journal because this is what I am really longing for in these days. As much as I'm learning, I still need frequent reminding and reorienting to what it looks like to walk with Him. How do we not run from suffering, but authentically embrace it when it comes? I'm still learning this over and over. The more I lean into God, the easier it becomes. When I embrace the *with-God life*, fear fades. I soak in the most repeated command written 70 times in the Bible, "Do not be afraid." Fear is losing its grip.

Every few months, I get more labs, more watching, more waiting to decide what to do next with this "stable" cancer in my neck. Is that even a real thing? The labs remain the same number for a year and a half. The scans tracking three spots they are watching have not grown. I'm beginning to believe that maybe this will stay dormant or be a thorn in my side keeping me in utter dependence. It's a good place for me to be. And I begin to consider writing about my journey.

---

20   Peterson, *"The Daily Message," pp. 448-450.*

I ask for prayer and support from friends and begin the long journey of scratching down the story He has been writing throughout this journey. The next day, an alert pops up on my phone saying I have new lab results from Kaiser. I resist the urge to open it that very second. I'm hushed into calmness by the great peace of His presence with me, even though everything in me wants to quickly click the New Test Results button.

I wait a few hours until I have a few moments alone to open the results. My heart pounds and leaps, and my eyes blink again and again to make sure I am really seeing this. The cancer is no longer stable. It's now "non-detectable." Non-detectable means the number is zero—a number I haven't seen in four years. I push out the nurse thoughts of possible lab error by remembering the words I read that very same morning in Mark's gospel story. I had written it down just hours before. Now, I weep tears of joy recognizing that He is in the details:

> "As Jesus healed He said... tell them your story, what the Master did, how He had mercy on you... Jesus blessed the life-long bleeding woman... daughter you took a risk of faith, and now you're healed and whole. Live well, live blessed... don't listen to them, just trust Me... whoever touched Him became well."[21]

I am in absolute awe of Him choosing this for me. I had come to a place of acceptance, and I'm not sure why

21   Peterson, "The Daily Message," pp. 81-82.

I doubted this kind of God-like ending to this chapter, perhaps because of the sprint-turned-marathon, but now I know I am living in a holy mystery. The leper, when he realized he was healed, turned around and came back shouting his gratitude, bringing Him glory, and I am trembling in thankfulness and wonder.[22]

This *leper* with a scar across the front of her neck is healed. I want to be that one leper who returns to give thanks. I go home and share my miracle story with my husband and the girls around the dinner table when we share our *high-lows* of the day. My high takes the cake tonight. He is at the table with me in the joy and the sharing of His wonder-working healing. We all cheer, cry, and hug each other tight.

The girls go pick flowers in the backyard in their matching pink nightgowns and bring them to me in a vase and write a precious note that says, "We are soooooooooooooooooooooooo happy mommy!" (And yes, that's the correct number of o's on that plain piece of paper that I treasure).

Later, I write to my friends near and far:

> Dear Fox-hole friends,
>
> When I began this journey four years ago, I had no idea how many amazing people would jump in to cheer, pray, love, provide, care, celebrate, cry with, carry, encourage,

---

22   *Luke 17:15-16*

and support our family like you have. People sometimes say that cancer is a gift, and now, I too can say I have seen the goodness of God in cancer... really. Like a parent who knows what is best for their kid, even when they just want to stay in their little sandbox. We often don't get to choose the chapter titles, but we get to choose many of the words that fill those chapters.

My labs for the first time in 4 years, showed the lowest detectable result possible of thyroid cancer. My ultrasound that had been showing 3 separate (0.5-0.7cm) slowly growing tumors, were down to only ONE (0.3cm) spot they could find. Heart pounding, tears flowing, mind swirling, wondering if God was doing a modern-day miracle of healing in me. For the first time it had not grown or even stayed steady, it was on the downhill trek to complete healing. I always believed he could do this but had come to accept that wasn't the chapter he was writing in me. I'm even feeling a little sad that I didn't believe more that He would do this. Still wondering what he is up to in all of this wonderful newness, but I receive the gift he is giving me today. And that is some deep heart, body, and soul healing, but I want the scars to remind me and help me not forget this etching of dependence it has brought. Perhaps the 0.3 sliver is there to remind me of that.

I believe that each of our own journeys has God's loving hand writing the story, and He is wooing us all to fall upwards to find our truest Life source in Him. To really find Him. He has titled the chapters, and I am just filling in the details, a good-hard, lovely practice.

So thankful for all of you! With a free and happy heart,

Janelle

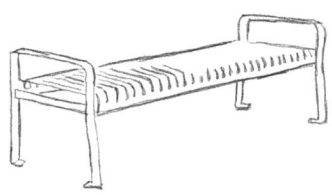

CHAPTER 9

LIVING IN THE
RECOVERY ROOM

*When my faith gets tired
and my hope seems lost
You spin me round and round
and remind me of that song
The one you wrote for me
and we dance...*

Bethel Music
"We Dance"

In this season of my body healing from cancer and my heart restoration, He also brings His renovation to the brokenness in my relationship with my mom, who is becoming invited into restoration and renewal by God's Spirit.

We have awkwardly walked through many years with disconnected hearts. On the outside it looked like a typical adult mom-daughter friendship, but it left us in need of major repair and grace in both of us. We shared recipes and photos of our lives, updates on new pets, occasional trips, and things that filled our days, but not meaningful heart space. There was a canyon of hurt and distance between us. We had become different people and didn't know each other anymore. What I did know of my mother, and what she knew of me, went only a few layers deep. A few years before my cancer journey, I started asking God to heal us. My daughter-heart longed to share soul space and for her to turn back to Him. After twenty years of walking away from her faith and her identity in Him, the God who recklessly pursues us, kept pursuing her. She finally turned back to Him, not with checkboxes, but with genuine heart-transformation that only He can do. She started asking questions about this "Gift of With" which I found. I couldn't wait to share more.

Healing between us was not overnight but a process through conversations—things said and some left unsaid. If you told me a few years ago our relationship would be what it is today, I am not sure I would have thought it was possible. Today we share the deepest heart pieces, the ways God is loving us uniquely. She is my biggest prayer warrior and cheerleader. Every Sunday we stand next to each other in church, worshiping the One True God who moves mountains, both dancing under the songs He sings over us. I am not sure I believed it could be this good, when the ground shook under me as a young adult. It is beyond what I imagined, just like God.

We spend nearly every 4th of July in San Diego, mostly to escape the Northern California heat, and also to celebrate our country's freedom watching fireworks on the USS Midway aircraft carrier. San Diego is also where my sacred ocean bench sits bolted to Sunset Cliffs. It is shaped like a cast mooring post for tying off ropes on a boat. This one anchors me and holds me steady. It's Freedom Day; and, I go to my post to meet Him again. How amazing to be here in person at this altar worshipping my Healer. I tell Him that He is true to the promise of being with me.

Feeling so known and so loved by the God of the world who made the ocean at my feet, yet He knows my name, even gives me a new one—*how is that possible?* I am humbled. Here is life-giving freedom. I bring prayers and burdens for others, and I lay them at His feet, wanting Him to whisper or yell if necessary to their souls, too. In case I'm tempted to think He might need my help, I'm reminded He is in control. I just need to seek Him with all my heart. It is such a quiet, peaceful place that speaks so loudly to my soul.

STILLNESS, SIMPLICITY, AND SHOWING-UP IS ALL I NEED TO DO.

He drops another gift into my heart when I get back to the car by playing the song that I started this chapter with. Stillness, simplicity, and showing-up is all I need to do.

Our family finds a spot at the patriotic concert in the park in Coronado. I break into dance when they play *Footloose*. The girls squeal with embarrassment, but I know they really love seeing me celebrate freedom, and they join in with wiggles and giggles. Then Scott and I go to the college date wall and soak in the lovely memories and the significance of this place. We thank God for the gift of healing and the freedom He brings. This restoration with Him is letting me taste eternity now!

He seems to be closing this season of cancer with healing and scars that will be pillars of remembrance and restoration. He brought me to a place of abundance and expectancy, of abiding and pruning, and being empty for Him to fill. What began on an ocean bench has been a life-altering journey of knowing His power, peace, artistry, warmth, refreshment, and so much more. This is a story much bigger than me. I am just a pebble on the shore. One story of a God who is personal and real and making all things new and restored.

Another full year of non-detectable cancer passes until a little bump up in my numbers adds some familiar concern. I've had so much practice holding my gaze on my Healer, but my heart still gets fluttery, just a bit less than before. Another 4th of July trip back to my favorite place, and I get to be back on the ocean bench; the timing ordained as the results just came a few days before. I ask if there is anything I should pray, since I am not sure. His Spirit answers, "Thy will be done," and I'm aware this is a peace-offering for me.

Here again, His written Word collides with His whispered words to my soul. It feels like a holy mystery and it brings indescribable peace. My doctor decides to do a re-measurement at the specialty USC lab. Results return again as "non-detectable." This becomes more confirmation for me of the repeated practice of not looking at the waves, but at Him who is control of them. I remember that is where my transformation and restoration is happening.

Webster's dictionary says that restoration is returning to a normal healthy condition, a fixing, a rehabilitation, redevelopment, renovation, mending, refurbishment. This is what God is continuing to bring beyond the bench and beyond cancer. But I still come back as often as possible to sit there at this holy place.

After more months pass, I sit on my bench yet again with a storm rolling in off the coast. The wind and the waves are whipping up, and I still go, with an umbrella, a dollar store poncho, my "Written Word," and my journal to write any whispered fresh messages to my heart.

A few minutes after soaking in the beauty and breathing deeply, I hear, "Mark 4," spoken over me. I'm not sure I heard right and not sure what will be on those pages. This is the first time I have heard a specific word like this. *Am I making this up?* So, I open to the page, and in red letters, "Why are you so afraid? Do you still have no faith?... even the wind and the waves obey Him!"

Okay, clearly, I am being shown something! I'm getting some real-life lab experience, once again sitting on the edge of an ocean cliff and seeing Him commanding the world with my very own eyes. This time my fears are more about the writing and sharing this love story, but I need the same reassurance. And, He knew. I keep reading on the same page, in red, "Go home to your family and tell them how much the Lord has done for you, and how He has had mercy on you... don't be afraid, just believe…."[23]

I want to jump up right then and run back, like the leper cured—to shout and sing and start writing right now! But, I need to stay here and write to my own heart. I clearly need to believe even more than I already did that He is so real. He *can* absolutely be encountered now on this side of eternity—but only by His Spirit that lives with me and in me, the Spirit of Truth, my Great Counselor and Divine Therapist. He's continually teaching me and reminding me of what He has already said to me, the new name He gave me, and the peace he continually brings. This fresh dose is for today. He knows I will need a new dose of it tomorrow, and the next day, and the day after that.

The Wonder-Worker has simply been doing what He always does, bringing me more restoration and more healing and life. It doesn't have to just be found in eternity; it can start now. He is so near and *with, with, with*… I am in wonder of Him choosing these particular details in the story of how He has revealed and is revealing Himself to me; and, I will bear witness to the realness of it. It is a life-giving gift, not just the gift of healing from cancer

---

23 *Mark 5:19, New International Version (Zondervan, Grand Rapids, MI, 1984).*

three times, but of brokenness in me, like broken sea glass being made smooth. I'm trusting Him now more than ever and knowing He is not done yet. I have been working in the recovery room as nurse for over 20 years now and I know now I'm living each day in my own *recovery room*. This reminds me of the word "blessing" that Andrew Murray speaks of the Apostle Paul's thorn, that he writes about in 2 Corinthians.

> "Paul's first desire was to have the thorn removed, and he asked the Lord three times that it might be taken away. The answer came to him that the trial, was the blessing-that through the weakness and humiliation it brought, the grace and strength of the Lord could better be manifested."[24]

When I get up from the bench and hop back in the rental car and turn on the music, the song, another one of our songs starts to play, and woos my heart again and again. It does not seem like a coincidence, but a Divine love note to my heart. It is a song about Him bringing joy from mourning, and I leave the bench feeling more loved and known every time.

I notice again the signs posted in the natural habitats along the ocean cliffs— "This area under restoration." It's a long, steady process of pruning and enduring

---

24 *Andrew Murray from Humility pg. 91 published Bethany House Publishers 2001*

the barren, withered feeling and waiting for new life to bloom.

I drive away thinking, *Remember this. It's a picture of your own soul.*

CHAPTER 10

THE REWRITE

I'd go hungry, I'd go black and blue,
I'd go crawling down the avenue.
No, there's nothing that I
wouldn't do,
To make you feel my love.

Bob Dylan
"To Make You Feel My Love"

My favorite childhood book was Shel Silverstein's *The Giving Tree.* I thought it was everyone's favorite until, after reading it to my girls for years, they confessed that it felt sad and depressing. I loved how the Tree gave and gave and gave, and still had more to give, even until the very end as a barren stump. The Tree captured my heart; I never thought about the selfishness of the boy. It was all about the amazing and selfless tree.

What makes my heart fully alive is giving to others. It's my superpower, one that has Amazon drivers showing up on my porch every other day, with those cardboard boxes full of surprises bringing Christmas cheer, even in July. I believe everyone should have a *gift closet* in their house. Gift-giving is my love language, and it's a great endorphin-producer for me, though definitely not for my practical, prudent husband. I have many gift-giving ideas pop in my head daily, which also makes runs to Target a joy ride. I love making people feel remembered, known and loved, and gift-giving is one way I have convinced myself this is the primary path to love. Unfortunately, the shadow and dark side of being an Enneagram Two is that the over-functioning, over-giving, generous-helper type, coupled with too much people-pleasing, can leave me depleted like Silverstein's tree stump. This ancient personality tool, exposes deep motives and why we do what we do. This tool helps you better understand yourself and people in your life.

I didn't want to be a Two. In fact, for months of my self-discovery journey, I pushed it away and tried to embrace my runners-up, Seven and Nine. But here's a tip to save a thousand dollars in counseling: the number you most don't want to be or that makes you feel the most exposed, is probably your actual number. The extravagance of Sevens and the zen of Nines seemed so much more fun than the needy, proud, codependent, hero-obsessed Twos.

Being reminded of my need to give up the Pollyanna-pleasing part of me is painful. But I also long to progress in surrendering and humbling. The more I see what needs to change, the more I have to wave the white flag and let God change me. As I start to write this story, I find myself stalled in the middle of a self-reflective intersection. Thoughts of who will read this, and how much of my heart I have to share and expose, paralyzes me. I think I just have writer's block, even though I am a nurse and not really a writer. I start

THE MORE I SEE WHAT NEEDS TO CHANGE, THE MORE I HAVE TO WAVE THE WHITE FLAG AND LET GOD CHANGE ME.

digging into the mess of my deeper self, and meet with a Christian counselor I find through my godmother's recommendation.

One of my Therapist's first questions is, "What does it mean to be fully alive and what makes you feel fully alive?" I take this homework seriously, like the discharge instructions after surgery. I start my *Alive List*. I jot down, "being present, feeling peace, being known and loved, music, unhurried evening walks with Scott." Oh, how I need these alive gifts.

I begin hoping all of this talk therapy will help me get unstuck. She gently comes alongside me to sort out whatever we find causing the blocks. Soon, it's time to look inward at my motives and core desires. She helps uncover so much of what is causing my unhealthy *Twoness*. I see that becoming good at helping others, even making it my career, has kept me from facing and fixing my own brokenness. Learning my Enneagram type, I see what is often my strength, can also be my kryptonite. This gift-giving thing helps me hide behind a false humility. Like C.S. Lewis says, "Humility isn't thinking less of yourself, it is thinking of yourself less." In my case, I tend to completely lose myself in being self-reliant and the effort to not be needy. My false humility is exposed, lost in the needs around me and neglecting the ones in my heart. Oh, I need another painful surgery, a kind of heart surgery.

But this *surgery* via therapy sessions, and the pain and turmoil it produces rivals the procedures required to take cancer out of my body. It is a daily process of removing unhealthy tendencies, like a surgeon removing pathogens. I need to go back to being "empty to fill," as Ann says.[25] It saddens me I am never done with this purging, but it is daily, even hourly, learning to surrender with humility to the Divine Surgeon of my heart. Taking out the cancer was just the warm up.

> "How do I die to self? Death to self is not your work; it is God's work... place yourself before God in your helplessness; consent to the fact that you are powerless to slay yourself; give yourself in patient and trustful surrender to God."[26]

25 Ann Voskamp, One Thousand Gifts (Zondervan, Grand Rapids, MI, 2010), p. 182.
26 Andrew Murray from Humility pg 84-85 published Bethany House Publishers 2001

Justifying my delayed obedience to share and expose the truth, I wanted to believe this was just a problem of struggling personality types. I can't deny my reluctance to share the soul details of the story, and even writing about it comes from fear of being unloved or needy. Can I stay on this treadmill of doing good things and keep avoiding what is brewing underneath?

As I wrestle over several months of counseling, again, I lose myself and who I thought I was. It is hard heart work. Constantly evaluating why I am doing what I am doing is exhausting. Looking at every motive and need makes me feel weak and disoriented. I go on a date with Scott in the middle of this season and cry over short ribs at Paul Martins, not knowing who I am and why I do what I do. It feels like the ground under me is cracking; and, I'm wondering where to stand. What I really need to do is to stay with this uncomfortableness, and not rush toward a temporary fix, invite the Lord into this space and let Him bring the healing I need, at Godspeed. I sense God teaching me something priceless, waking up the deadened, ignored places of my heart I've covered over with distracting duties and overdoing. And if I can just stop and stay with the painful realization for a bit, the beauty of what He can do with dead things may make me more alive than ever before.

When the counselor asks, "What makes my heart come fully alive?" It reminds me of the St. Irenaeus quote about how "the glory of God is seen in a person fully alive." This has captured me for years, this phrase written down on several pages of my journal and etched on my heart. I finally pause to ask the question, *How do I live fully alive and awake?* Not the self-fulfillment kind of vacation fantasy that seems to disappear as fast as it comes, but the kind where I'm filled with the steady and sustaining knowledge; I'm fully engaged, alive, and awake in this living experience with God—in this life He has given me.

Again, I sit on the quiet bench by the pond and look on the pages of my Bible where Jesus asks over and over, "What do you want?" I hear the same beckoning question whispered to my heart—except I can't seem to answer. *I want what You want,* I think. That is so Two of me. What do *I* want? I've been living unaware of the deeper desires He has put in my heart. *Wake up, self!* And not my false self, but the true, undefended me.

I take care of half-awake people all day in the recovery room. I have been in a conscious sedated state myself. Learning about myself has helped me know more of Him, but it feels like it has stirred up unwellness in me—insecurity, weakness, motives, shadows; and, I sometimes doubt this *heart surgery* is worth it. But on a bench, He reminds me again He is with me and bringing more wholeness in me. "Deep knowing of God and deep knowing of self always develop interactively. The result is the authentic transformation of the self that is at the core of Christian spirituality."[27] *That's it!* I can't just learn about God alone to live a transformed and whole life. I need to keep digging out this *self-cancer* that I've allowed

---

27   *David Benner, The Gift of Being Yourself (InterVarsity Press, Downers Grove, IL, 2015), p.31.*

to slowly spread in my heart. This is what I want, to really wake up from living half asleep in everyday moments.

Honestly, being a Two, others' needs and desires are easier to deal with, just as it seems easier to pursue knowing God than knowing myself. Even having needs brings a sense of shame, as though I'm being selfish. So, I always push them down, diminish, minimize, and hide them in the shadows, putting on a face of self-reliance and going over-the-top in giving to others.

I like to focus on the good and this is why I've always clung to a Pollyanna disposition. I don't like looking at pain or struggle, current, past, or future. I know other people have it worse than me, so I need to take the weight off their shoulders. I can get by; I'm fine—not because I'm perfect, but because I don't deserve to be the priority. I tell myself I can get around to fixing myself later. When I would work a 12-hour ICU and ER shift, I often forgot to eat or even go to the bathroom until I got home. I thought this made me a good nurse. How can I live like Mary in a Martha world, while so tangled up in the busyness of helping others?[28]

In the midst of these new counseling sessions, I read in my "homework" book and find the jaw-dropping question, "What have you learned about yourself as a result of your experience with God?" And then, "What do you know about God as a result of genuine encounter with yourself?"[29] I answer with having subtle but major hero issues.

---

28   Luke 10:38-42
29   David Benner, The Gift of Being Yourself, Intervarsity Press Downers Grove, IL 2015, p. 31

Within a few days of this revelation, our small group at church, the one we like to call "Family-You-Choose," decides to help a refugee family from Syria. The word "help" immediately makes me want to sign up, of course. We get some training on how to interact culturally and personally with the family. The experienced worker tells us to "not be the hero" to them, as it might seem easier to do things for them rather than teach them or let them do for themselves. I feel something like scales falling off my eyes, suddenly seeing the way I so often move to *give* by over-giving, which can cripple people and create dependence I am not even aware of.

I'm struck by the revelation that I have often *craved* giving in this way to distract from my own need. I am plunged into even deeper self-doubt and feel like I'm pulling up in *Dysfunction Junction* once again. On the surface, I feel my motives have always been to make others' lives easier, to lighten their load, to give and serve. But I can see the core motive now, and it makes me squirm. I want to be esteemed, approved, praised, and to be the hero who shows up to help. This is how I look for love.

After seeking more wisdom from my godparents and therapist, I decide to participate in a guided Scripture meditation called Lectio Divina, the ancient spiritual practice of seeking God through scripture, meditation, and prayer. The verses on this day are about a woman crippled for eighteen years. I can't imagine the pain and isolation, but Jesus saw her and healed her instantly with a touch of His hand. Like He did so often, it brought controversy, being on the Sabbath.[30] Our guide asks us to picture ourselves in the story, and instantly I'm this woman's friend helping and holding her arm while she's hunched over. Then with gentle and kind conviction, I sense Him showing me I want to heal her, that I think it's up to me to be her hero. I feel gut-punched in the most loving way. I cry and confess, again, this over-helping tendency in my heart. Something breaks free in me that day. I never again want to be choked by the false burden of being so put together that I am isolated by pride.

Being the "hero" doesn't bring me what I long for—true closeness and love. Learning to let God do His thing is the boundary I am continually drawing and redrawing, then drawing again. Sitting with my wise therapist, I tell her I need her to help me get back into writing this story. She does some more amazing digging, and I see I'm also stuck with fear of rejection. No hiding from full honesty here.

I enter some new pruning, seeing how much of what I worry about and strive for is not really up to me. When I practice surrender and healthy detachment, I live freer. When I think of the words of these pages being a *gift* for whoever needs them, I can press forward. I can do gifts! This is what sets my heart free, the more I can practice this healthy giving and helping. The way He loves me and teaches me to give better life gifts makes me want to rewrite *The Giving Tree*, with apologies to Shel. If I did, I would be the tree who simply let the boy ask for help, and then reminded him where his true source of help

---

30   *Luke 13:10-17 (NIV)*

comes from. I would also remind myself I am not the tree, only God is.

I could be there to cheer the boy on whenever he came back and needed someone who believed in him. I would teach him how to plant and grow and harvest his own fruit. I might remind him of who created me and him, and that the One who brings the sun and the rain makes us grow. I'd tell him the story of how the deepest roots find water sources others don't know anything about. Maybe I'd point out the happy face scars carved in my trunk and what they've taught me, and with those journey scars, I'd just keep doing what I was created to do—blooming, giving shade with my green leaves, and surrendering to the changing seasons year after year, until I finally went to be with my Maker.

Actually, I think I'd also include a postscript about attaching a hummingbird feeder. Having a candy bowl always full for visitors is still on the *okay list* for Twos.

After six months of working through all this heart pruning, I take a walk by the lake and listen to a conversation with Dallas Willard and John Ortberg on living in union with God. They ask, "What could be more amazing than just being *with* God for the day?" *With* God! *And then I hear* Him answer in my head and heart, "Seeing the gift of God's Spirit living *with-in* me every day." *Yes! Wow!* Not just on benches, or in my good times, but *all* the time, even in my struggles and disappointments. Now that is the gift! Letting that sink in for a moment or two takes my breath away. Can you get goosebumps on your heart?

Knowing God by experiencing Him with and with-in me, would definitely make my heart feel fully alive. I can experience Him by paying attention, seeking Him out, and pausing on benches. This is how I can partner with awakening more of His Spirt in me—in the everyday moments. It only takes remembering I have the eyes to see, the ears to hear, and the heart to feel, even when there's not an oceanfront bench.

Even on simple walks, I am expanding my listening territory now. Habbakuk says, "Look at that man, bloated by self importance—full of himself but soul-empty. But the person in rightstanding before God through loyal and steady believing is fully alive, really alive."[31]

---

31   Peterson, "The Daily Message," p. 1445.

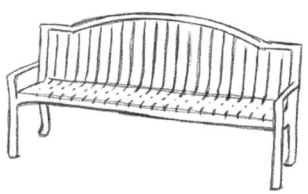

CHAPTER 11

JUST BE

Sometimes I gotta stop,
Remember that you're God
And I am not,
So...

Thy will be done...

Hillary Scott
"Thy Will"

For more than a decade, I have wondered why so
many of us blatantly disregard one of the Ten
Commandments. We hold all the others up as non-
negotiable tenets to living a virtuous life—do not kill, do
not blaspheme, do not steal, or lie, or cheat. Got it. But
something happens at the Fourth Commandment. It's
as if we suddenly hear static. "Remember the Sabbath
day, to keep it holy." In our workaholic, overscheduled

culture, this one command in God's list of life-giving rules, seems hardly noticed—and rarely practiced—even in our Christian culture.

I've had seasons that felt so weary that rest seemed like a luxury I could never afford. Forced Sabbaths have certainly come by way of cancer, cancer, and cancer again, five weeks of bedrest with a high-risk pregnancy, and the occasional flu. I usually come through those times giving thanks for rest, acknowledging how good it is to slow down and even vowing to do more resting. But not long after I recover, I seem to slip right back into the rat race of the world and Sabbath as a spiritual discipline is the first thing to drop in my overscheduled life.

There is a simplicity about rest that feels refreshing, but not knowing how to live in a rhythm of rest in the day to day and week to week is literally killing us.

Wayne Muller says, "If we do not allow for a rhythm of rest in our overly busy lives, illness becomes our Sabbath—our pneumonia, our cancer, our heart attack, our accidents create Sabbath for us."[32] This has been messing with me, but I have only been thinking about it, not actually doing anything about it. When I am forced to stop in my tracks, I do not greet the opportunity with joy, but with the irritation of major inconvenience. Is it even possible to have a weekly rhythm that includes a whole day to rest and delight in God?

I think about it—I'm sure many of us do—but then I always hit the ground running, and don't stop again

---

32   As quoted in Ruth Haley Barton, *Sacred Rhythms (InterVarsity Press, Downers Grove, IL, 2006) p. 131.*

until I have to. Emptying my life in order to fill back up with Him—wasn't that the lesson of cancer? We get to practice this rhythm each and every week by emptying our lives of schedules, of toil, of sports, and to-dos, and even of serving others and striving for goodness, for just one day. God doesn't just give us permission to do this—He commands us to do this. But, we don't or we can't.

Everyone around you understands when you have an illness. If you've just had surgery, birthed a child, or are ingesting nuclear radiation, rest is fine. Not so much when you are saying no to so many good, even important things, just because you're *religiously* setting aside a day a week to rest.

He made the heavens and the earth in six days and rested on the seventh. In the days of Exodus, not observing this law brought a death sentence. Today, by not observing it, we incur a death sentence of a different sort. We are slowly killing ourselves, running ourselves ragged to do more and more, all because of FOMO (fear of missing out). We fill our time doing anything but resting from the craziness and the false productivity god we serve.

In my early morning time with Jesus, I read that Sabbath is supposed to be a denial of ourselves (our own ideas, Leviticus 16:31) and was created for us as a get-to, not a have-to, a covenant (a commitment or bond), and a sign of the relationship between us and our Creator. Also, Sabbath is a reminder to know and remember who He is and who we are (Ezekiel 20:12). To even know who I am and who He is, I need space in my head and my heart. Not having any unscheduled time one day a week keeps me spinning all the wheels all the time and losing perspective in the turning. They are all good things scheduled on the calendar and so I buy the lie that my disobedience to this command is justified.

In Jewish days, Sabbath was a day of gathering to hear the word of God (Acts 13:44). Jesus often was teaching and preaching on the Sabbath at the synagogue. In coming to Him, we find rest for our souls, for real. So how do we rest in God? Jesus seemed to do this every day, not just on the Sabbath. It was an attitude, a lifestyle, a true emptying of self and opening to God, so I am not "sightless among miracles," (as I read in a Jewish Sabbath prayer) just last night.[33]

I am back at the Mercy Retreat Center to write and to dig into this rest God has laid on my heart. It's quiet and still and simple in my retreat room. I read Eugene Peterson words,

> "An accurate understanding of Sabbath is prerequisite to its practice: it must be understood biblically, not culturally. A widespread misunderstanding of sabbath trivializes it by designating it 'a day off.'… However beneficial, this is not a true sabbath but a secularized sabbath. The motivation is utilitarian: the day off is at the service of the six working days. The purpose is to restore strength,

---

33   *https://www.soulshepherding.org/sightless-among-miracles/*

increase motivation, reward effort, and keep performance incentives high… The side effects of shored-up family harmony and improved mental health are also attractive… Sabbath means quit. Stop. Take a break. Cool it. The word itself has nothing devout or holy in it. It is a word about time, denoting our nonuse of it, what we usually call wasting time… Not-doing. Being-there. The sanctification of time. We don't have any rules for preserving the sanctity of the day, only the commitment that it be set apart for being, not using. Not a day to get anything done but a day to watch and be responsive to what God has done."[34]

When I return home, I set myself a goal, write it out, and pin it up in the kitchen for all of us to be reminded, for one day of the seven in a week:

STOP.

QUIT.

FIRE-YOURSELF FOR THE DAY.

PRAY.

PLAY.

GO TO CHURCH.

---

34   https://www.soulshepherding.org/sabbath-as-praying-and-playing/

BE WITH GOD.

BE WITH PEOPLE YOU LOVE.

BE UNPRODUCTIVE.

BE.

Sounds delightful until I really try to practice it, and then try to get the family to join in, and give up technology addictions for a day. It exposes control and pride and idolatry in all of us. On my walk that morning, I hear Peterson say that the age of technology access trains us to think we can do a lot more than we can. It has to be a deliberate decision, a conscious stopping we can't just drift into, like my forced Sabbaths up to this point. We simply select a day of the week and quit our work and just be. We will need also to protect it as our inner instincts will oppose it; so will our screen-addicted culture. It is not a day that proves its worth

OUR CULTURE PRIZES AND REWARDS PRODUCTIVITY, EVEN IF IT KILLS US IN THE PROCESS. IT ALWAYS WANTS MORE OF US.

or justifies itself. Entering into empty, nonfunctional time is difficult. We have been taught that time is money, which our culture values above all.

Any friendship worth having is deliberate. Sabbath is a choice which takes planning, thoughtfulness, and commitment. As I practice it, each Sunday helps foster my friendship with Jesus, my family, and my "family-you-choose." I know I must practice choosing the dreaded word *no* and learn to just be. Be-Still-And-Know-That-I-Am-God for one day a week. Slowly, over the next few months stumbling around to make changes, it helps me remember I am really not in charge on the other six days, afterall. I think maybe this is me learning to be Mary in a Martha world. Our culture prizes and rewards productivity, even if it kills us in the process. It always wants more of us.

> "If you watch your step on the Sabbath
>
> and don't use my holy day for personal advantage,
>
> If you treat the Sabbath as a day of joy,
>
> God's holy day as a celebration,
>
> If you honor it by refusing 'business as usual,'
>
> making money, running here and there—
>
> Then you'll be free to enjoy God!
>
> Oh, I'll make you ride high and soar above it all."
>
> Isaiah 58:13-14[35]

We begin this soul pilgrimage as a family, and soon we're doing well in about half of the Just Be List. They seem totally on board for a new rhythm of rest and

---

35   Peterson, *"The Daily Message," p.1499-1500.*

unhurried space and pace. But I still wonder how we plan for it, put boundaries on it, and protect it without it becoming religiosity, eventually weighing us down. Human nature can so easily take what God intends as life-giving and turn it into life-sucking duty and religious obligation. Honestly, this is one of the reasons I have hesitated to make this command part of our family life. I fear even the appearance of legalism, a reminder of much of my childhood. And yet simply drifting along and expecting it to magically happen doesn't work either.

Plus, I completely ignore a weekly day of rest being an actual *command* of God. I know anything He commands is for my own good, so do I trust that? He reminds me it is about being *with* Him, and Him being *with* me in a day of playing, and as much continual praying as I can manage. It isn't supposed to be drudgery.

I believe with all my heart Jesus was and is Sabbath in a person.

The Book of Matthew says, "There is far more at stake here than religion…If you had any idea what this Scripture meant—'I prefer a flexible heart to an inflexible ritual'—you wouldn't be nitpicking like this. The Son of Man is no lackey to the Sabbath; he's in charge."[36]

Later, I read in Hebrews, "And so this is still a live promise. It wasn't canceled at the time of Joshua; otherwise, God wouldn't keep renewing the appointment for 'today.' The promise of 'arrival' and 'rest' is still there for God's people. God himself is at rest. And at the end of the journey we'll surely rest with God. So let's keep at

---

36   Peterson, *"The Daily Message," p.458.*

it and eventually arrive at the place of rest, not drop out through some sort of disobedience."[37]

As we continue along Sunday by Sunday, I come to see how learning this rhythm of rest is a conduit for experiencing eternity now on this side of heaven. It's in the daily, the weekly gift of unhurried life and rest. This is a taste of the Eden I keep longing for, a timeless peace—perhaps even built into our DNA from our Creator. And I read in the words of Andy Crouch from his book *Playing God*, "Sabbath is a circuit breaker for idolatry."[38] I feel released to look at more of what I may need most: to become more aware of my idols of efficiency, of productivity, of over-giving, and feeling like it's all up to me—that pride-bound thought of trying to control all my fears of disappointing people.

These are just a few of the idols I need to surrender. I need to remember it is who we are, not what we do, that matters in the end. *Do I really believe this?* The way I live each week, with my time, gives an answer.

So now the question is, how can I go from this aching awareness I'm not doing this, to making Sabbath part of our regular family life and rhythm? How do I avoid making it a list of rules we end up resenting, while missing the authentic experience of true *with-ness* with our Creator? Can I *make* it happen? Or is this not just more of me trying to help others? This is so upstream in our

---

37   Peterson, "The Daily Message," p. 257.

38   *As quoted by Amy Julia Becker in "Are There Any Christians Who Take a Day of Rest Anymore?," Christianity Today website, Oct. 2013, https://www. christianitytoday.com/amyjuliabecker/2013/october/are-there-any-christians-who-take-day-of-rest-anymore-some.html*

current culture, where every day looks the same around us, playing organized sports so our kids don't miss out on friendships (and the promise of future scholarships), so many games and then God-help-us championships, and working so we don't get behind on all the emails, work, church activities and serving. Good, important things become ways to neglect our deep need for rest.

As I sit on the porch pondering all this again, I recall how last fall Scott and I went to Nashville for a long weekend. We stayed in a second-story loft close to Vanderbilt University and the hospital. It was buzzing with life and noise with the businesses below us. Not quite as crazy as Broadway downtown, of course, but a constant white noise, at least until Sunday morning. On Sunday, it was clearly noticeable—no noise. The quiet and stillness was such a contrast. As a lifelong Californian, I was shocked to find that apparently, the South still observes a partial *break* for businesses on Sundays until two in the afternoon. Now, I don't know how faithfully or not everyone actually observes it, but it was refreshing to this West Coast girl. I wondered how to weave this rest back into our life in California. *Is it even possible?* Probably not, I reluctantly conclude. We return home; and, I pick up where I left off, no rest, no break, just keep going, going, going.

But something pulls at me and I decide to dig deeper with a few conversations at work with my Jewish and Seventh-Day-Adventists friends. Their Sabbath experiences sound a bit legalistic as well, with a list of work-arounds and *rules overload*, too. In the early

Jewish days, I learn the "Sabbath was not merely a day to recharge one's batteries; it was a day that the rest of the week could not survive without," according to Rabbi Abraham Joshua Heschel.[39] It was a day of remembering, blessing, leisure, good food, family, and of course the part that can be its demise, regulations. "All the regulations can be boiled down to two principles: do not create and do not be lord over nature, just for one day a week." (summarized from Talmud Tractate Shabbat by Sharon Ayala)[40]

According to Dr. Tilden Edwards,

> "The principle involved in deciding what is work here is not so much the physical nature of an activity, but its purpose. If its intent signifies human mastery of the world by the purposeful and constructive exercise of intelligence and skill, then it is *meluchah*, work, which violates the restful intent of Sabbath time to recognize our dependence on God as ultimate Creator-Sustainer."[41]

I'm beginning to think perhaps my struggle with Sabbath is again about surrender. Only when forced to rest through cancer and isolation retreats have I learned to surrender. How do I change to willing surrender?

---

39   https://www.pointloma.edu/resources/theology-christian-ministry/
losing-sabbath
40   Ibid.
41   Ibid.

What does it take? What will it cost me? I'm starting to believe it will actually be the things that don't matter anyway, and in return, losing them may give me more of what my soul really longs for: goodness, true rest, and restoration.

Sabbath is slow, simple, unhurried stillness. This is what I know I need as a regular rhythm for my life. It was a glimpse of the intentionality necessary to fight for this life-giving practice that is so opposed. I had planned this getaway to do some writing at the retreat center. It nearly took an official act of Congress for me to get here for just thirty-six hours. And, I had to say, "No," to a dozen good and fun things and to another dozen *shoulds* which I carry all the time. I almost threw in the white flag, but I knew I should and needed to go. Interference and obstacles coming from all directions made it feel like it wasn't worth the effort, and I rarely even make time for retreat space often.

But I knew I should start taking this command as essential to my soul health. And after sleeping nine hours last night and feeling like time has halted to a snail's pace once again, the soul awakening has already begun. It *is* so worth it. To practice regular Sabbath will take the same focus and determination as it did to be here. Planning, protecting, and advocating for our souls is a must. The harder it is, the more important it is. I don't do this very well. It is hard and upstream.

So, despite everything, and my fears of legalism, I know I need to encourage all of us, my family and friends, to regularly leave the diamond lane on the freeway and take the offramp to the road leading to rest for our souls. I haven't yet found any benches on the freeways here in California. I think they are only on the side roads, off the beaten path. And, my favorite benches have views of the magnificent ocean that He alone could have created.

Jesus says, "For what will it profit a man if he gains the whole world and forfeits his soul? Or what shall a man give in return for his soul?... Are you tired? Worn out? Burned out on religion? Come to me. Get away with me and you'll recover your life. I'll show you how to take a real rest. Walk with me and work with me—watch how I do it."[42]

I briefly wonder if it is a coincidence that my ache for rest and Sabbath has roots in the name He gave me on the bench. But I know for certain, deep in my soul, that it is God moving in my heart as I learn to rest in Him.

> "A third component to biblical Sabbath revolves around delighting in what we have been given. God, after finishing his work of creation, proclaimed that 'it was very good.' God delighted over his creation. The Hebrew phrase communicates a sense of joy, completion, wonder, and play. This is particularly radical in a culture like ours, both secular and Christian, that is 'delight deficient.' Because of the way pleasure and delight have been so distorted by our culture,

---

> many of us as Christians struggle with receiving joy and pleasure. On Sabbaths we are called to enjoy and delight in creation and its gifts... on Sabbaths God also invites us to slow down to pay attention and delight in people..." [43]

Finally coming to this deep conviction that my heart will not let go of, because of the life-giving gifts found during my forced Sabbaths. I want to keep this conviction burning in my bones. Our "delight deficient" culture, with more anxiety and depression than ever before, could use a dose of "profound joy and happiness" found in this soul-kindness practice. I am finding the realness and nearness of Jesus in it. I am not sure I can survive the rest of my weeks without it. I need this kind of rest. I need to be more present and with my people and with Him.

He often healed on the Sabbath. He *still does*. He rebelled against our human regulations for Sabbath to show us things which had nothing to do with our worthiness through productivity. It was always simply about peoples' availability. Rest brings healing and His *rest-oration* to my weary heart.

Now I can pray sincerely with the words, "... This idea of Sabbath will require a lot of change in the way I am living my life. Lead me, Lord, in how to take the next step with this. Help me trust You with all that will remain unfinished, to not try to run your world for You.

---

43   Peter Scazzero, *Emotionally Healthy Spirituality (Zondervan, Grand Rapids, MI, 2017) pp. 157-158.*

Set me free to begin orienting my life around You and You alone."[44]

44   Scazzero, *Emotionally Healthy Spirituality*, p.163.

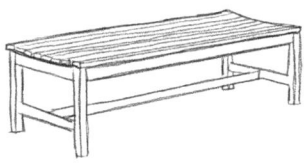

CHAPTER 12

HOW IT'S SUPPOSED TO BE

All the things You have done,
tell the story of love…
This is not the end of the story,
This is only just the beginning…

Thrive Worship
"Greater Things"

"*What do you want?*"
I remember hearing those words whispered to my heart on a bench a few years ago. I really couldn't answer without a *Sunday School* reply: "I want what You want."

It sounds like a good answer, but great counselors ask great questions. This question was from The Counselor that has a zip code in my heart. It doesn't go away with shallow answers. The deepest desires, the ones placed in me by Him, get clouded with a million other things. I couldn't even give Him an answer reflecting my own heart. Of course I wanted to know Him more and deeper, but I wonder, *Have I squashed any earthly desires in my heart so fully that I no longer even feel when I get disappointed? Am I protecting myself and just playing it safe?*

As I'm pondering all of this, I get an image of myself walking around in a fog and never awakening to my truest desire. I clearly want Eden, as I have said over and over again, but the details of my desires *unique to me* are hazy gray. Like Solomon, who desired and asked for the greater good of wisdom and was given much more because of it, I want my answer to be wise.[45]

I think I am afraid I may settle for less if I speak what I desire. I fear it will be out of my shallowness.

One of Scott's and my favorite authors and mentors says,

> "We are desire. It is the essence of the human soul, the secret of our existence. Absolutely nothing of human greatness is ever accomplished without it. Not a symphony has been written, a mountain climbed, an injustice fought, or a love sustained apart from desire. Desire fuels our search for the life we prize. Our desire, if we will listen to it, will save us from committing soul-suicide, the sacrifice of our hearts on the altar of

---

45   *2 Chronicles 1:11*

'getting by,' The same old thing is not enough. It never will be."[46]

I remember my godmother telling me the story of desire welling up in her after its dormancy. Someone asked her what one of her dreams was, and she said she couldn't answer between all the demands of motherhood and home and career that she was doing daily. It unsettled her to not be able to give a really profound answer. She watched my godfather live his dreams of fishing in Alaska on epic trips which brought life-giving moments with God and His creation. Later she finally answered the question with her dream to learn to play the harp. Her answer even surprised herself, and she was not sure where it had actually come from. She pressed into that desire and God has done things beyond what she ever imagined. She now plays the harp as music therapy in hospitals at the bedside of patients and brings Eden to them in their sickness.

Desire is linked to love, and love to motive. What do I love? How do I love? Why do I love? Jesus commands us to love Him and love others, and we don't get extra credit for loving the hard to love. I do know I can't will myself to do this in an authentic way with my own strength.

Maybe like learning to love my mother-in-law.

When I was first dating Scott, his mom was not a fan of me. I was used to being liked, or at least accepted, so I did not know how to navigate this rejection. It was, of course, complicated with all the details of

46   John Eldredge, Desire, (Thomas Nelson, Nashville TN, 2000) p. 11.

her own story—of her hurts and the dysfunction she suffered. Over several years of simply trying to love, one day I suddenly went from just miming the motions of loving her to truly loving her. And, it came to me through a dream.

She was not far from death, and there were so many years of drama—her quirky, funny-sad behaviors—and when she was becoming even harder to love, I once again asked God to show me how to love her. But this time with more urgency.

I had a dream that we were in what seemed like heaven. A large group of people mingled around. At the edge of the group, I glanced up and saw her. She was content, healthy, and had a wholeness and radiance about her. I grabbed my chest and gasped, "Ah, this is who you were supposed to be!" I woke up that morning and vividly remembered the dream and the emotion I'd felt. I only knew her in her hurts and unhealthiness; and, my dream changed the way I loved her from that point forward.

If only we could love people for who they *really are supposed to be*, who they are beneath all they've suffered, see who they are one day becoming, who they were always created to be, and look past all the brokenness, I believe we could change the world.

So often I get stuck worrying about how I'm being seen or being treated. What I am learning now about desire is that there's a deep connection to *asking* and simply making your wish known to ourselves, as much as to God or anyone else. I need to ask for help to love.

When I read through the Scriptures, I note over and over again the word *ask*. "Ask, ask, ask… Seek and you will find."[47] There is humility and *surrendering* in the asking. My stubborn heart cringes at the very thought of so freely expressing my *need*, but I believe the asking part of desire is about humility.

Jesus reminded me recently in Matthew's letter,

> "Don't bargain with God. Be direct. Ask for what you need. This isn't a cat-and-mouse, hide-and-seek game we're in. If your child asks for bread, do you trick him with sawdust? If he asks for fish, do you scare him with a live snake on his plate? As bad as you are, you wouldn't think of such a thing. You're at least decent to your own children. So don't you think the God who conceived you in love will be even better?"[48]

So if you'll excuse me here, let me be direct with what I know I desire. I desire the words on these pages to be a gift to my daughters, so they will get to know my heart. And most importantly, so they will know deep in their hearts that the God who made them knows them, loves them, sees them, and has a new name for them, as well. I hope they'll be compelled to see God *with* them in all the chapters He is writing in their very own lives. And I want to love the people around me for who *they* were

---

47   *Jeremiah 19:12-14 (NIV)*
48   *Peterson, "The Daily Message," p. 450.*

created to be, to make them feel fully loved that way, and for whoever reads this love story to believe they can find Him for themselves, not because of my testimony but because they have a special bench somewhere, too. And I want to love God with every layer of my heart, and mind, and soul, through to the end of this life and on into the next. Just being with Him is my deepest desire every day. I do also long for help in all of this and for more dreams to remind me and reawaken this desire. I'm not sure if I will ever learn to play the harp, or fish in Alaska; but, I most strongly want to stay awake to any fresh desire He puts in my heart.

I know I will continue to long for Eden, as we all will, and to the moments and movements of God on a bench or anywhere. I know I'll be letting Him sing over me, to let those songs move me closer to Him, and to share His *Genius Playlist* with others. I know it is Him who will do the truest filling of my heart, to be the *delight* He made me to be. But most of all, I'll continue longing for full restoration for our broken and hurting world and all in it, until it looks like what Louis Armstrong described.

> "I see trees of green,
>
> red roses too
>
> I see them bloom
>
> For me and you
>
> And I think to myself

HOW IT'S SUPPOSED TO BE

What a wonderful world"[49]

That's Eden, how life is supposed to be. Trees of green, Giving Trees that speak of the best Gift-Giver. Until we get there, I hope you'll keep looking for benches with me and clinging to the only gift that provides a taste of eternity here and now—His Presence, His *with-ness*.

Him with-in, and with us. Always.

---

49   *"George David Weiss & Bob Thiele, What A Wonderful World," recorded by Louis Armstrong, 1967, ABC Records.*

ACKNOWLEDGMENTS

Gratitude is one of my favorite spiritual practices. It opens my heart to more of God and to the goodness being given.

I am grateful to so many for cheering me on to put this story to paper. My first person to tell me to write and (in her authoritative voice) advocate that I have a voice, was Denise Belden. And she is now in heaven, but I can't wait to see the smile on her face when I tell her about this book.

To my husband Scott, who motivates me to always reach my potential and believes in me and this story as much as I do.

To my daughters, who walked this journey with me as little girls and are now young, strong, *beautiful* women on their own journeys. I love being with you. I pray, most of all, you are finding this incredible gift yourselves.

To my family and our "family-you-choose," you know who you are, and so do I. I'm so grateful for you. Thank you for praying for me to get this done over all these years of delay, through all my excuses, and for being my hospital-bed people.

To my mom who gives grace way beyond what she has been given. You are my best cheerleader.

To my godparents who have shown me this gift time and again and pointed me in the right way to keep finding it.

To my editor, who is way out of my league. We have nearly fifty years of life together; plus, I am named after your mom, who is also a nurse, so you kind of had to say yes. Also, to my fine-tuning professional and screenplay writing best friend-sister, who makes Restoration Hardware out of Costco things in my life. I'm grateful to the team of people who know way more than I do in this publishing world and have championed getting this story to where it is today.

And finally, to all the musicians who gave the gift of music to crack open my heart through your offering of beauty and art that became a deep part of my story. Your songs have become souvenirs I collected; postcards I kept from the journey. They are the playlist of my soul. I first captured them in my journal and then scattered them about on these pages. Thank you for sharing your stories with me to remind me of the way God sings over us.

To the many other writers whose books have etched themselves on my heart, with new ones still coming along—especially Eugene Peterson. Your way of paraphrasing timeless truth helped heal my heart. I'll thank you when I get there.

This is my story.
This is my song.
Praising my "with-me" friend-of-my-soul
All the day long!

A GIFT FOR YOU

A few *gifts* for you the reader if you desire to grow deeper in your own spiritual journey, and learning how to live into the *with-God life* more. These are a few of the timeless spiritual practices and resources that have become a lifeline for me along the way. These practices have been woven into the story, and some are included here for gifts to be opened by you. Your friendship with Jesus requires time, patience, and practice, just like any personal relationship, and that is The Gift!

THE GIFT OF MUSIC

A Spotify playlist created to go along with the chapters and songs in the book. The Psalms are songs and prayers that are a wonderful place to connect with God, by reading, reflecting, and making them into your own prayers. Bono and Eugene Peterson talk about the gift of the Psalms on the link (next page). Tim Keller has a Daily Devotional called, "The Songs of Jesus" through the

Psalms. Create your own playlists that help you connect and encounter Jesus and play them often.

Spotify Playlist

Bono Interview

Tim Keller Book

THE GIFT OF BEAUTY

Get outside, exchange coffee dates for going for a walk dates, plus it only costs you time not money. Scott and I have been taking after dinner walks since our first year of marriage and it is one of our best marriage tips. Walking and talking are a form of therapy and help our minds file and process things. Jesus walked and talked with his people all through His life, and He still will walk with us now. He usually goes at 3mph-Godspeed. Slowing down to find the beauty!

Godspeed Video

THE GIFT OF SURRENDER

Daily practice a posture of surrender to God, praying or worshiping with palms up helps our souls catch up to our bodies, we are mind, body, spirit. Surrendering to God, everyone and everything, is a practice of "Benevolent Detachment" (Wild at Heart, John Eldredge) that helps me learn how to care, but not carry, the burdens of my heart. The Pause app has guided prayers to help get you started and keep you going in this.

Pause App

THE GIFT OF HUMILITY

Ask, ask, ask God to speak to you. So many times in the Bible, we are urged to ask God. He does not force His friendship upon us; it is an invitation. This humble practice of asking is the window in which His voice will come. A yearly read of Andrew Murray's, Humility, will be a lifeline for your soul.

Andrew Murray Book

THE GIFT OF THANKFULNESS

Keep a gratitude list going, what is good, ways God has answered prayers in the way you prayed, or in the unexpected ways. Many times you will see Him in the details of your life that will make you be in wonder of Him! Writing these down in a journal will help you in the now, and in the rearview mirror. It also will give you eyes to see the goodness of God and feel His love more. This is the best way to start your day and also your daily time in practicing the presence of God, and make as breath prayers throughout the day.

Gratitude Journal   *Breath Prayers*

THE GIFT OF COMMUNITY

Go to church. Find a church with your people: show up, serve, and stay when it gets hard. It is like family—it will have ups and downs, and things you connect with, and like, and don't like. Be a helpful participant and not a consumer. Be in a small group, where you are really known. Join one or start one, and stay committed in the mess. You are so welcome to join our thriving church, or jump into one in your own community.

Bayside Church

THE GIFT OF LEARNING

Find a mentor, someone who you know walks with God, and learn from them. It may be an author, podcaster, preacher, parent, or friend. Our godparent is one of our mentors and has amazing resources here to explore. Keep learning about who Jesus is, and His character. He is who will save you, redeem you, and rescue you.

Mentoring Sacred Arts   *Beautiful Outlaw*   *The Problem of Jesus*

THE GIFT OF LISTENING

Reading the Bible is an active experience of listening to God. When you are not sure where to start reading the Bible, a great place to start are The Gospels (Matthew, Mark, Luke, and John), Psalms and Proverbs, in whatever version you are most comfortable with. I like reading different versions, it keeps it fresh, especially if you have grown up reading and hearing about the Bible. The Message version is a paraphrase that is modern. Before you start reading, it is a good practice to start with a short prayer inviting God into your time of reading and learning, and even picturing Him near you. Maybe even light a candle to remind you of His calm warm Presence with you while you read. Listening to the Bible, and having God's Word read over you is also a special way to experience the Living Words of God. Write in your journal things that made your heart pang, and then ask Him if He has anything to say to you. Sit in the stillness, and it may come immediately, or even later in the day, or the week ahead. When you sense it is His voice, write it down. It will always be in the character of who He is, and in complete alignment with His written word, The Bible.

Dwell App   Bible Study   Gospels

Praying you find your own benches, ocean views, and with that the sweet friendship of Jesus on your own journey!

These gifts and more can be found at
www.thegiftofwith.com

www.ingramcontent.com/pod-product-compliance
Lightning Source LLC
Chambersburg PA
CBHW070328130626
46556CB00007B/2771